PROTECTING CHILDREN AND YOUNG PEOPLE

Effective family support
Responding to What Parents Tell Us

PROTECTING CHILDREN AND YOUNG PEOPLE SERIES

SERIES EDITORS

JOHN DEVANEY
School of Sociology, Social Policy and Social Work, Queen's University Belfast

and JULIE TAYLOR
School of Health and Population Sciences, University of Birmingham

and SHARON VINCENT
Social Work and Communities, Northumbria University, Newcastle

Effective Family Support
Responding to What Parents Tell Us

Cheryl Burgess
Honorary Research Fellow, Centre for Child Welfare and Protection, University of Stirling

Ruth McDonald
Corporate Policy Officer, Falkirk Council

and

Sandra Sweeten
Manager, Kelvinside Academy Green Forest Nursery, East Dunbartonshire

EDINBURGH ◆ LONDON

First published in 2018 by Dunedin Academic Press Ltd.
Head Office: Hudson House, 8 Albany Street, Edinburgh EH1 3QB
London Office: 352 Cromwell Tower, Barbican, London EC2Y 8NB

IISBN: 978–1–78046–073–4 (Paperback)
            978–1–78046–586–9 (ePub)
            978–1–78046–576–0 (Kindle edition)
ISSN: 1756–0691

British Library Cataloguing in Publication data
A catalogue record for this book is available at the British Library

Typeset by Makar Publishing Production, Edinburgh, Scotland
Printed in Great Britain by CPI Antony Rowe

CONTENTS

	Acknowledgements	vi
	Author Biographies	vii
	Foreword	viii
	Introduction	x
Chapter 1	Theories, models and the evidence base for family support	1
Chapter 2	Remembering the basics	17
Chapter 3	The art of assessment	33
Chapter 4	What do parents say they need?	53
Chapter 5	Building family resilience	75
Chapter 6	Are we making a difference?	88
Chapter 7	Conclusion	102
Appendix	The research studies	111
	References	114
	Index	122

ACKNOWLEDGEMENTS

Firstly, we are grateful to all the parents and carers who told us about their experiences and whose words are recorded in this book. We also wish to thank the many practitioners who arranged for us to meet with the families.

Thanks are also due to Brigid Daniel, who encouraged us to write this book, and to Sharon Vincent for her advice and mentoring. We would like to acknowledge the support given by Nick Burgess, Kelly Stone, Peggy Shatwell and Sarah Ridley.

We dedicate this book to Sandra Graham, whose wisdom and dedication inspired us all.

.

AUTHOR BIOGRAPHIES

Cheryl Burgess is an honorary research fellow at the University of Stirling, where she worked for thirteen years as a researcher. She was previously a local authority social worker.

Ruth McDonald is an award-winning social worker with extensive experience managing family support services in the third sector. She now works as a policy officer for a local authority.

Sandra Sweeten has primarily worked in the field of social care and Early Years. She currently works as the manager of Kelvinside Academy Green Forest Nursery, based in East Dunbartonshire.

FOREWORD

Never has it been more important to value and preserve family support services – the pressures on parents are enormous. Far too many parents in the UK are working long hours with low pay, are on tenuous or no contracts, struggle to find decent housing and bear the brunt of brutal austerity measures. These pressures, coupled with associated personal issues such as mental health problems, isolation and relationship breakdown, can have profound effects on parenting and on children's wellbeing. The availability of non-stigmatising, compassionate support can make an enormous difference to the whole family.

However, family support services are themselves falling victim to austerity measures and associated cuts in public funding. All too often projects that do survive are constrained by short-term funding, specific models of practice, targets and narrow requirements for specific outcomes.

All projects, of course, aspire to be effective, but the focus on specific prescribed 'outcomes' must not come at the expense of what parents most need. This book provides invaluable insights into the best way to create welcoming, empathic and effective services for parents who are struggling.

The authenticity of this books lies in the extent to which it is informed by the views of parents – both fathers and mothers. The book is underpinned by extensive research undertaken over many years, which has gathered the direct views of parents and children about what kind of support helps them best. The consistency of the messages from so many different studies, undertaken in different settings and contexts over several years, is striking. Many of these messages coalesce around getting the basics right. This research is also informed by the authors' practice wisdom and knowledge of the underpinning theory about what helps parents. This is important, because it must be acknowledged that parents may not always agree that they need help with their parenting, or they may not recognise the impact of their behaviour on their children. Establishing empathic connections with people to enable them to begin to benefit from services is crucial. Many of the parents who contributed to the research underpinning this book have reflected on their own ambivalence about seeking help or being referred for help, and their views are the more powerful because of that.

The authors do not promote one specific model of intervention, rather, the evidence from the research that is drawn on suggests that effective family support needs to be informed by principles underpinned by theory that can be applied in a range of settings using different models. The book offers an accessible overview of two main theories – ecological theory and family resilience. Ecological theory provides a framework that encourages practitioners to identify the layers of factors that may be affecting parents from the wider structural and social pressures through to the intimate experiences of the individual. Parents themselves may be so focused on the proximal issues that it can also be helpful for them to gain the broader perspective that an ecological approach brings. Family resilience theory is essentially hopeful, in part because it encourages self-efficacy, and is therefore important to share with parents. More recently, resilience theory is being augmented to recognise the extent to which challenging oppressive conditions can improve resilience, too.

The book appeals to our common humanity; in particular, the focus on getting the basics right reminds us all that the parents who are struggling need the same kind of respect and courtesy that we all want from services. It is hard for any of us to ask for help from strangers, and we all share a fear that we will be re-buffed – not taken seriously or belittled. None of us would like receiving help in a building that is not fit for purpose and that seems shabby and dispiriting, and none of us would like to receive help from practitioners who are not themselves supported in their work.

Professor Brigid Daniel

Dean of School of Arts, Social Sciences and Management,

Queen Margaret University, Edinburgh

INTRODUCTION

> 'Family support – it sounded hopeful, I was quite excited – it was what I needed. It's one thing to get given leaflets about parenting but that's not enough.' Parent, study H

The origins of this book

Most parents and carers need help from time to time with the demands of caring for children. Many of us are lucky and can call on the advice and support of friends and family; there are some parents and carers who cannot. It should not feel 'shaming' or 'nerve-wracking' to ask for help with being a parent, and yet that is what we have heard consistently from parents and carers in the course of our combined seventy years of work in this area.

This book will draw on our practice experience in providing what is broadly known as family support. For the purpose of this book, this means the support required for parents to care for and nurture their children. It will also make use of the findings from multiple research studies, undertaken by one of the co-authors over a twelve-year period as a researcher, which explored the effectiveness of support for families living in a range of situations. These studies included parents with new babies and those struggling with teenagers; families involved with the child protection system; and kinship carers coping with complicated family circumstances and dynamics. A full list of the research studies from which the views of parents were drawn can be found in the Appendix. Each is identified by a letter code, which we use in the main text to show which study the quote from the parent was drawn from.

In this book we use the term 'parents' to include all adults who are providing primary care for children: for example step-parents; grandparents; those providing kinship care; foster carers; and adoptive parents. In society today, there are many different types of family and parenting arrangements. Children are cared for in shared-care arrangements, by same-sex couples, lone parents and by family and friends. Some of these families may be managing particular difficulties, including complicated family dynamics. Parents who have physical or learning disabilities may have their own challenges to face.

There are numerous definitions of 'family' – one dictionary describes it as 'a social unit consisting of one or more adults together with the children they care for' (www.dictionary.com), although, of course, there are many families without children. The family unit has always had a fluid form, with adults leaving and joining other families to form reconstituted families, but we are increasingly moving away from the traditional form of a family led by a male and female parent. There are research centres and programmes across the globe that explore family life and the effects on children of these different family structures (Centre for Research on Children and Families, University of East Anglia; Australian Institute of Family Studies; and the Organisation for Economic Co-operation and Development's (OECD) *Doing Better for Families* research programme(2011)). In undertaking support work with families, practitioners must be open to different family structures and include any family members who are important to the child.

Some of the participants in our research and practice, whose views form the core of this book, were step-parents, lone parents, part of a same-sex parenting couple and kinship carers. Some had disabilities or were experiencing poor mental health, and some were misusing drugs and alcohol as a way of coping with past and present difficulties. While there were particular challenges associated with having a disability or misusing substances, the parents' individual circumstances meant that their experiences of parenting were all different, regardless of any label that could be used to describe them. The parents did not categorise themselves in this way and so, in this book, we do not differentiate between 'types' of parent; their experiences of receiving family support services were surprisingly uniform, whatever their circumstances.

We found that, despite families' diverse situations, a number of common themes emerged from our work, and our aim in this book is to share what we have learnt with other practitioners and researchers. These themes explore the general approaches that parents told us were helpful and that made receiving support from professionals more acceptable to them. We will build on these themes by suggesting practical actions, which those working with families can use in their day-to-day work. Many of these will be familiar to some of our readers; however, we hope that, by emphasising what parents found helpful, we will play a part in inspiring new or renewed enthusiasm for the important task of providing support to those who are finding it hard, for whatever reason, to care for their children in a safe and nurturing way.

Research and care service inspections now rightly include the 'user' view of services (Care Inspectorate,2017; Ofsted, 2017; RQIA, 2016). It follows that these views should also be taken into account when planning services and training staff in the skills required to deliver them. Wherever possible in this book, we will use the words of parents and carers to describe and illustrate what they told us they found helpful. And, given what parents frequently say about professionals' use of jargon and specialist language and the problems they have understanding this, our intention is to write this book in the day-to-day language used by families.

It is important that practitioners make themselves clearly understood when talking with parents and carers, and in explaining, at the outset, why they are involved with their family. While most practitioners will do this as a matter of course, it can be easy to slip into the use of social work, health or education terminology, especially when other professionals are present. Many of the tasks practitioners undertake to support families are simple and practical but are sometimes lost in a cloud of jargon and vague terminology in assessment and review reports. The language used is often understood by other professionals, but parents say that they are often left feeling excluded. This book is aimed at those providing support to families and not directly for parents themselves. Nonetheless, we hope that, by using everyday language to describe approaches and activities, it would also make sense to parents and carers.

In the course of our research and practice we have consulted many children and young people about their experiences and views of receiving help from professionals. However, the focus of this book is on the views of parents and, while we recognise the importance of children's views, we do not have space here to include them in a way that would do justice to the richness and insightful quality of what they told us. That would require another book. We are keen not to exclude children and young people completely, however, and have given a flavour of what they said in Chapter 6, where we look at how we can measure the effectiveness of family support.

Family or parenting support?

We have chosen the broader term of family – rather than parenting – support to describe our subject. There are two main reasons for this. Firstly, our work with parents has shown us that their ability to care for their children may be affected by practical, social and emotional difficulties, and help will be needed with some or all of these. In effect, help with parenting may be just one aspect of the support required. Secondly, many parents said that being told that they needed assistance with their 'parenting' implied that their skills in this area were lacking and made them feel inadequate and stigmatised. This can lead to some parents 'putting up the shutters' or becoming defensive when professionals become involved with their family.

> 'There's something about being told you need help with your parenting. It sort of labels us as bad parents. There are difficult things for everyone about being a parent.' Parent, study B

Parents considered that the use of the term 'family support' was more acceptable to them and felt less negative. As many parents lack confidence or are wary of involvement with professionals, the words we use are worth careful consideration.

Family support

So, what do we mean by family support? It tends to be loosely defined and can be used as a wide 'catch-all' term for working with families, so that its meaning becomes difficult to pin down. While the term is used in the design of national and local policy and in developing services and practice, the general way in which it is described is seen by some writers as a weakness (Canavan *et al.*, 2016). To Canavan *et al.*, the generalised nature of its definition does not lend itself to a shared understanding of what it means in practice, although an advantage of this is that it allows for a flexibile approach when helping an individual family.

One formal definition of family support is:

> ... both a style of work and a set of activities that reinforce positive informal social networks through integrated programmes. These programmes combine statutory, voluntary, community and private services and are generally provided to families within their own homes and communities. The primary focus

of these services is on early intervention, aiming to promote and protect the health, well-being and rights of all children, young people and their families. At the same time, particular attention is given to those who are vulnerable or at risk (Dolan *et al.*, 2006, p. 16).

Or, as a parent told us:

'Our support worker has helped in lots of small ways, with advice, listening, practical things which have added up to make a big difference to our family.' Parent, study H

We like this definition by Ann Buchanan (2002), because it recognises that all families need help at some time and that it can be varied and practical in nature:

Supporting families is about the 101 things that can be done by friends, neighbours and social care professionals to help families manage the essential task of bringing up children (Buchanan, 2002, p. 253).

In the same way, we believe that family support, when provided by professionals, is sometimes best offered by more than one person – it may take the skills of practitioners from different agencies to meet the needs of the family. We have learnt that both children and adults value services that work with them both, together or in parallel, so that, for example, social or emotional support provided for children is supplemented by help for parents on how best to care for them. This must be balanced with families feeling overwhelmed by the involvement with their family of too many professionals:

'It can be a bit confusing and stressful when we have too many appointments to keep and we feel bounced about between so many different services and staff. They keep changing all the time or someone else is sent if ours is off.' Parent consultant, study F

We heard that duplication of support can be counter-productive, especially if different advice is being offered by the various professionals involved.

Parenting support

Clearly, parenting support is an important aspect of family support. Definitions of parenting support tend to be more narrow than those of family support, although, in many ways, their aims are similar – that of equipping parents to provide for their children's needs. In their review of the international evidence of what works in parenting support, Moran *et al.* (2004) use this as their working definition:

> Parenting support is any intervention for parents aimed at reducing risks and promoting protective factors for their children, in relation to their social, physical and emotional well-being (Moran *et al.*, 2004, p. 21).

Importantly, they add that 'parents must themselves feel supported by the help or services they are offered'. However, they also point out that a parent feeling supported is not necessarily the same as the support being effective – in other words, that it has led to improvements in children's everyday lives. Moran *et al.* (2004) point out that this definition does not describe what parenting support actually looks like in practice, given the many forms it can take. We discuss models of family support in Chapter 1.

Fathers and other male carers

While the term 'parent' should equally mean both male and female parents, most research about family support is based primarily on that provided by mothers and female carers. There is increasing recognition of the important role of fathers and other male carers, in looking after children and providing them with positive roles models. Research tells us that practitioners do not always take full account of the positive as well as the negative aspects of the father's role and the potential for the father to provide nurturing care for their children (Taylor and Daniel, 2005; Featherstone, 2009; Clapton, 2013). There is evidence that the quality of early childhood play with fathers directly affects teenagers' feelings of self-worth (Lewis and Lamb, 2007). Positive time spent with fathers and a close supportive relationship is directly linked to better outcomes for children as they reach adulthood, regardless of whether the children live with their fathers (Asmussen and Weizel, 2010).

In practice terms, there is growing evidence about the best ways to involve fathers in family support work, where this is beneficial for children (Maxwell *et al.*, 2012). There are also an increasing number of services designed to support them in their caring role (Scourfield *et al.*, 2014). Male carers were involved in the research and practice settings we draw on for this book. Their views about how individual professionals and services had supported them and valued what they, as parents, were providing for their children, are included. In using the word 'parent' to attribute quotes, we do not differentiate between males and females although the context in some cases makes this clear.

Pressures on parents

It is important to recognise that individual families do not exist in a vacuum – they are affected by governmental policies on employment, welfare payments, housing and health provision. There may be a range of pressures that have a bearing on family life, and this may include financial worries and poor or insecure housing, not to mention the expectations which society places on children and young people – and, as a consequence, their parents or whoever is caring for them – to own the latest technology, clothes and other possessions.

It is clearly an impossible task for family support workers to take on the society-wide inequalities that can affect how children are parented. However, practitioners must try to see the individual family's situation within this wider context. Later on, we will describe what parents have told us about the practical help support workers, including social workers, Early Years staff and health professionals, can provide, which helps to overcome the financial and material disadvantages many of them face.

While parents can, of course, make their own decisions and choices about how they care for their children, we must remember that there may be broader factors that influence the extent to which they are able to make the most of the support offered to them. Parents are influenced by their own family histories and personal experiences, as well as ongoing life 'events' such as illness, bereavement and changes in close relationships.

Policies aimed at helping families

Over the last twenty years, UK governments have developed a number of strategies and policies aimed at supporting families in their care of children. These include those provided on a universal basis, and others for families who require additional help. These are too many to list, but examples include *The Early Years Framework* in Scotland (Scottish Government, 2009); *Improving Lives: Helping Workless Families* (Department for Work and Pensions, 2017); *Delivering Social Change for Children and Young People* (Northern Ireland Executive, 2014). In England, the 'Troubled Families' programme, funded by a £448 million government grant, aimed to 'turn around' the lives of 120,000 families with 'multiple and complex needs' (Day *et al.*, 2016).

At a local level, public services provide and commission services that aim to meet the needs of families, in particular those who require extra support, although these are always limited by budget constraints. There has also been a move towards the use of validated parenting interventions and programmes, aimed at parents in the general population and including families seen as 'vulnerable' (Holloway and Pimlott-Wilson, 2014; Marryat *et al.*, 2014).

Do these interventions and programmes work? While they appear to make a difference to some families, in the course of our practice and based on research feedback from parents we suggest that a 'one size fits all' approach will not be enough for some families. This is backed up by research that tells us that some families require more than a structured programme, delivered over a limited time period (Statham and Biehal, 2005; Daniel and Rioch, 2007). Such a programme may form part of the support offered, but individual, tailor-made support and the human factor – a relationship between parent and support staff based on empathy, trust and honesty –is often what makes the difference. In this book, we aim to provide evidence from parents we have spoken with about the importance of basing support on this approach.

The focus of this book: parents' views of family support
The main aim of this book is to describe what parents said to us about the support they received – what was helpful to them and their children. On the whole, this is about the help practitioners gave them, as adults, to parent their children and to improve other aspects of their lives, which were influencing the care they gave them. Most forms of family support also include direct support for children. There are useful practice-based books that describe creative and effective ways of providing support for children (Tait and Wosu, 2013; Emond *et al.*, 2016; Clark and Moss, 2016) and for children and their families together (Sawyer and Burton,

2016). We do not detail these in this book, and so suggest that practitioners refer to those for ideas about working directly with children. Having said that, some of the family support work that we describe in Chapter 4 does involve children undertaking activities together with their parents: for example, learning to play and trying out new ways of talking with children.

Who is this book aimed at?

This book was written for social workers, Early Years practitioners, health visitors, youth workers and family support workers – in fact, all those who are offering direct support to families. We hope it will be helpful to those who are training them and those being trained. We are particularly keen for our book to offer ideas to those whose direct time with families is limited due to high workload and organisational demands. Academics with an interest in the views of parents as service users may also find their views insightful. We recognise that different parts of the book may be of interest to different people – we hope that readers can dip in and out and find the sections most useful to them.

Content of the book

This book primarily aims to offer practical advice and suggestions for approaches to and ways of offering support to parents, based on what they told us. However, we start by giving some context, and in Chapter 1 we suggest possible theoretical bases to the work –ones we have found helpful and easy to explain to others. A theoretical basis for the work is important and can serve as an ongoing reminder to professionals of what they are aiming to achieve in supporting a family. By regularly examining what, if anything, is changing as a result of the support and, if necessary, re-assessing their aims and strategies for doing so, they (and the families) will be getting the benefits of reflective practice.

Chapters 2 and 3 explore the first stages of family support being offered, from the position of those who are receiving rather than providing it. We consider the views of parents and, wherever possible, use their own words to do so. We go 'back to basics' and look at the importance of first meetings in setting the tone for what follows – parents were clear about what made this positive, or otherwise, for them. In Chapter 3, we also attempt to cast a different light on the art of 'assessment', with parents' thoughts about how the use of visual 'tools' can lead to assessment being more meaningful, useful and interesting for them.

Chapter 4 looks at what we consider to be the three cornerstones of family support: building on parents' knowledge; boosting their confidence; and improving their skills. These are illustrated with examples of how this can be done in a positive and enjoyable way, which parents described as being most effective for them. In Chapter 5, we look at the ways in which family learning and resilience can be strengthened to make a real difference for families in the longer term.

Chapter 6 tackles the challenge of measuring the effect that our support of families has had on the everyday lives of children and their parents. This is increasingly required by organisations when undertaking future planning, in order to assess both the changes in children's circumstances and the effectiveness of services. In Chapter 7 we conclude with our thoughts about practitioners' knowledge, skills and confidence, and how these can be shared to develop a workforce equipped to help parents. In essence, this could be described as a nurturing support worker who is able to nurture parents and families because they themselves feel valued and supported by their employers. This should not be an unreasonable aim!

CHAPTER 1

Theories, models and the evidence base for family support

Introduction

In this chapter, we outline the theoretical background which we have found helpful in understanding and explaining support work with families. We look at the reasons for having a theoretical background to our work. We discuss models and frameworks of family support and what we know about the evidence of the effectiveness of family support as a way of improving children's lives. This chapter is different from the ones that follow because, by its nature, it is not based on what parents told us and does not include quotes from them. In that sense, it has a more academic tone than later chapters. We hope, however, that it explains the content and ideas behind the theories that we use to underpin our work in a way that makes sense to practitioners. Our intention is to enable them to relay this to others – primarily to other professionals but also to parents, in situations where this would be helpful. Our aim in this chapter is to provide background to the provision of family support before we move on to the chapters that cover the more practical aspects of the work.

Theoretical background

What is a theoretical framework and why is it important?

A theory presents a systematic way of understanding events, behaviours and/or situations (https://obssr.od.nih.gov; accessed 19 January 2018). We may have personal theories or hypotheses about what types of support families might find helpful, based on our own experience, instincts and common sense, but, by themselves, these are not enough. We might think that, in theory, practical help and supportive relationships might encourage parents and other family members to develop improved skills and, in turn, help them to nurture the children they care for. However, while these all play a part in our work with families, a tried, tested and widely acknowledged theoretical framework, which we can cite as a basis for our work, will carry more weight when explaining to others what we hope to achieve, and why. A framework that brings together knowledge from different sources – for example, from sociological and psychological, as well as practice backgrounds – and provides a structured way of understanding them is an important part of working in an evidence-based way. Practitioners can also find such a framework to be a practical aid in their work with families.

The trick is to be able to refer to and explain our chosen theoretical approach in situations when we need to lend professional credibility to our work while also finding a way to demystify it when talking with families *et al.*.

Payne (2005) refers to three types of social work theory:

- what social work is – the nature of welfare, why we have it and how it should be delivered;
- how social work is done – practice theories about the best ways to help someone;
- those which offer knowledge to social work about the world (sociology, psychology – which can be used to inform understanding about things).

We are concentrating on the second one of these, that is, practice theories that seem to offer an effective approach to family support. These theories have an evidence base to support their effectiveness.

Why is it important to have a theoretical and evidence base for family support work? Firstly, as we explain below, having a theoretical framework, which 'sits behind' their work with families, can help practitioners to examine what they are doing on an ongoing basis to try to ensure that the support provided is purposeful and stays 'on track'. Secondly, practitioners may find themselves in situations where they are actively challenged about the methods they use in their interventions with families and the rationale for using them. When this happens, they must be able to explain these clearly. For example, in some instances even intensive and skilled family support work can prove ineffective in helping families care for their children, and children may become subject to legal proceedings. Practitioners may need to contribute to the court process by way of a written report or by providing verbal evidence. This will probably involve giving a clear description of which 'interventions' or support families were offered, and why. An explanation of the theoretical framework for the support, and the evidence base of the models used, may help to make the submission more convincing. Evidence about why the interventions were unable to prevent the need for a child to be removed from their parents' care will also be crucial.

Using theory to explain support work with families

In their book *Understanding Family Support: Policy, Practice and Theory*, Canavan *et al.* (2016, p. 12) note that 'as yet there is no distinct family support theory'. They acknowledge that there are some benefits to this flexibility, mainly in terms of the scope this gives for different styles of practice and individualised types of support. However, they also argue that, if family support is to be seen as an important component of the child welfare agenda, it needs to develop 'sufficient theoretical coherence' and a 'single, strong, synthesising position' on what it means, and why. They suggest that being able to articulate 'clear positions' for the work would give those undertaking it a firmer basis for doing so.

Canavan *et al.* (2016) describe five 'positions' within which they consider that family support work should be located. They place importance on employing reflective practice in family support work and the use of four main theories to 'frame and inform' it. These are described as: social ecology; resilience; social support; and social capital. These concepts have also been used by other academics in the field to understand and develop a framework for family support (e.g. Jack, 2000).

The theories we use

The theories we have found most useful in thinking about family support work are ecological theory, otherwise known as social ecology theory, linked with that of family resilience. We think that these two, taken together, include the two other main components referred to by Canavan *et al.* (2016) and other writers, namely social support (or social network development) and social capital.

These theoretical perspectives have, in recent years, been developed to form the basis of the main models of practice employed by child and family social workers in the UK. Some of their main components have been incorporated into assessment and planning frameworks, such as the *Getting it Right for Every Child* (GIRFEC) approach in Scotland (Scottish Government, 2012), with its use of the 'My World Triangle' to assess a child's circumstances in the round, and the *Framework for the Assessment of Children in Need and their Families in England and Wales* (Department of Health, 2000). The *Understanding the Needs of Children in Northern Ireland (UNOCiNI)* assessment follows a similar framework (Northern Ireland Executive, 2011).

These national practice frameworks, which include policies and guidance, at either national or local level, have been developed with the aim of safeguarding children's welfare, where possible by early identification of children who may be at risk of harm or neglect. These include strategies to try to ensure that all services, including universal ones, which are involved with families work together to support the child and their family or carers.

It is possible that the theory that sits behind what is now everyday practice for many professionals has led to the former, to some extent, being subsumed. The boundaries between theory and practice may have become blurred, and it could be argued that this is not necessarily a bad thing. However, in order to recover the theoretical bases for family support and child welfare work, it may be necessary to rewind slightly and disentangle them from the practice frameworks, so we can see again how they fit together.

A good place to start may be to remind ourselves what a theory actually is – that is, a possible explanation for a situation and what might help it change. Practitioners need to continually reassess the aims of the actions required to support the family, and whether what they are doing is contributing to meeting those aims. They must try to focus on the component parts of the theoretical framework as a backdrop to the work they are doing with the family. In the case of an ecological approach, which we outline below, this means working to minimise risks and stressors and to increase support and strengths of families at a number of levels including the immediate family, their wider networks and the broader 'community'. Practitioners can use the structure provided by the theoretical frameworks to gather the evidence that shows how and to what extent the actions of the practitioner and family are meeting the aims that the theoretical approach aspires to affect.

An ecological approach

The theoretical framework on which this approach is based stems from the work of Urie Brofenbrenner (1979) and his ecological theories of human development, later added to through the work of Belsky in the 1990s (Belsky 1984; Belsky, 1993). The ecological approach considers social interaction to be shaped by the nature and dynamics of systems which interact with one another – all of which are influenced by the particular social context in which they take place. This approach is often used as a way of assessing individual child development and the factors that influence the child's well-being.

Belsky (1984) used this framework and other research findings to devise what he saw as the key determinants of parenting. These were: parental personality and psychological well-being, their systems of support (including their relationship with any co-parent) and also, to a lesser extent, the characteristics of the child they are caring for. The two key points he drew from this and which he saw as interlinked in either a positive or negative cycle, were: that parents who are psychologically secure and well-supported will be more likely to cope with difficulties in caring for children than those under stress and with little social support; and, secondly, that parents' personality and well-being can influence their ability to find and make use of social support, the availability of which will, in turn, have an impact on the well-being of the parents. This development of the ecological approach is useful to us in providing a theoretical basis for family support.

Following on from Belsky's work, other writers have looked at the relationship between the social environment and parent–child characteristics (e.g. Quinton and Rutter, 1988; Jack, 2000) and have concluded that the relationship between the two is not straightforward, and the interacting influences will have different effects on individual families. Some parents can overcome and compensate for disadvantages, including poverty, more easily than others. Much depends on the personal histories and emotional development of parents themselves, the impact these have on their parenting and how they can best be supported to change any aspects of this which are unhelpful for their children. These all need to be taken into account when using an ecological or holistic approach to designing support for a family.

An ecological approach to family support takes into account the different factors that influence parenting and how the children in the family are cared for. It does this with reference to the different circles, or 'levels', within which family life happens. These levels include:

- the immediate family: those living in the household and non-resident parents (if in contact with the child);
- extended family and significant friends, including any others who provide childcare;
- neighbourhood contacts, nurseries, schools, clubs and groups.

By pinpointing the supports that are an aid to parenting, the stresses that hamper it and by identifying the resulting protective and risk factors for the child, this framework offers a full picture of the family's situation, and a plan of support can then be drawn up, aimed at addressing any highlighted gaps. Thus the theory is that, by taking a holistic or ecological approach to the family's situation, the practitioner is better equipped to provide the family with the most effective supports.

The theory and the framework around it give the practitioner the structure that enables them to tailor their support and to make plans (which must be adaptable) to carry this out. It also helps to identify aims against which success can be measured – usually the health and well-being of the child as well as more skilled and confident parents.

Family resilience
The concept of resilience as it relates to the whole family developed from that of childhood resilience and the use of a resilience-based approach in working with children and young people. It also stems from the concept of 'coping' and the development of coping strategies for families facing adversities. It is considered that, by building resilience in parents (or whoever is caring for the child) who are under pressure, their children's resilience can in turn be enhanced (Erickson and Henderson, 1998).

There are many definitions of resilience – one of the most widely used is that coined by Luthar (2005, p. 6): 'a phenomenon or process reflecting relatively positive adaptation despite experiences of adversity or trauma'. Much research has been undertaken into the factors associated with resilience, which can be categorised under the main headings of (a) psychological/dispositional attributes; (b) family support and cohesion; and (c) external support systems (Friborg et al., 2003).

The theoretical basis and practice approaches to working in a resilience-based way with families are less developed than those with children.

Building resilience in children has been explored by a number of writers (Gilligan, 2001a; Daniel *et al.*, 2011). There are also useful practice guides to working with children using a resilience-based approach, including the series written by Daniel and Wassell (2002a; 2002b; 2002c), who use the six key domains of resilience-building as a structure within which to undertake this work. A new approach to resilience has been developed by Angie Hart and her 'communities of learning' collaborators, which is based on building resilience as a community, especially in those areas which experience social deprivation (Hart and Aumann, 2017). Their 'Boing Boing' project has developed a resilience framework and tool for use by shared groups or communities of families and practitioners.

The individual resources considered key to family resilience are similar to those identified for children, notably: intelligence, knowledge, humour, hardiness, good health, sense of mastery, good self-esteem (Walsh, 1998; McCubbin *et al.*, 1999). In addition, it has been identified that 'resilient' families or those which respond well to crises are those who have shared goals, communicate well (adults and children) and are willing to change (Daly, 1996).

The work of McCubbin *et al.* (1999) in developing the Resiliency Model of Family Stress, Adjustment and Adaptation included the identification of a typology to try to explain why some families cope with stresses more easily than others. They outline six main dimensions of family characteristics which can be assessed using a number of standardised measures. They concluded that a strong family bond, adaptability, strong leadership, good communication and the ability to problem-solve were key factors for resilient families. However, we must remember that, in some situations (e.g. where there is domestic violence), the continuation of the existing family unit may not be in the best interests of some of its individual members, and that sustaining that particular family unit and building its resilience may not be a desirable outcome (Hill *et al.*, 2007).

In Chapter 5 we make some suggestions about how practitioners can encourage the development of family resilience. One of the aspects we outline is widely recognised and can be considered as a theoretical perspective in its own right – that of building social support networks. In some respects, this also incorporates the concept of 'social capital' (Bourdieu, 1986). Social capital is a term now widely used to describe the resources (actual or virtual) which we gather as a result of our relationships with others (Canavan *et al.*, 2016). Social capital is most often defined using three categories: 'bonding' social capital, if it involves a relationship with people in similar circumstances to our own; 'bridging' social capital, if a member of our social 'network' has contacts within another network; and 'linking' social capital, if a member of our 'network' knows someone in a position of power, such as a politician. Given that one aim of intervening to support families might be to help them to access support when they need it, building a family's social capital could be seen as integral to this (Jack and Jordan, 1999).

It is worth noting, however, that social networks are not necessarily a force for good (Jack, 2000). They can be a source of stress and conflict, and should be developed with care and discrimination, as far as this is possible.

Two other concepts associated with resilience are also useful for us in relation to family support – those of resilience chains and turning points (Gilligan, 2009). Resilience chains can take place when building resilience in one area leads to enhanced resilience in another: for example, when a person's involvement in activities leads to improved confidence in meeting people and making friends. Turning points can occur when opportunities arise for a family member and they feel able to make the most of it, perhaps because of greater feelings of self-confidence or self-efficacy. Even seemingly insignificant incidents can lead to important changes and chances for development (Gilligan, 2001b).

The concept of resilience is not without its critics – some dislike the onus it puts on individuals to develop coping mechanisms in order to face adversities which may be caused by structural inequalities within society and which should be addressed at that level (Daly, 1996). It has also been recognised that, sometimes, an outward show of resilience or apparent coping can mask internal distress (Luthar, 2003). Perhaps most importantly for our use of it in the context of family support, there are those who argue that resilience-based approaches have much similarity to, or at least draw to some extent, on other perspectives such as attachment and ecological theory. They suggest that some interventions or service models that are labelled as resilience-based approaches are essentially very much the same as those developed under the umbrella of other strengths-based perspectives (Yates and Masten, 2004). That is why, for us, the use of ecological and family resilience, as underpinning theories, go very much hand-in-hand.

Models of family support

In the introduction to this book, we offered possible definitions of family and of parenting support. It is noticeable that information about models of parenting support is more available than those that describe family support. This may be partly because a number of parenting programmes have been evaluated in order to be accredited. There are a number of comprehensive reviews of evaluated parenting programmes which offer guidance about their effectiveness and about the types of approaches that are considered helpful for parents and their children (e.g. Barlow, 1999; Moran *et al.*, 2004; Barrett, 2003). These studies also provide evidence about effective approaches to wider family support, and include feedback from those who took part in the programme about what they found useful in encouraging them to 'stick with' the support and utilising the advice given in the long term. The importance of the development of a therapeutic relationship between practitioner and parent, and of pitching information and ideas about parenting at the right level for parents, were noted (Barrett, 2003). These principles can be applied to wider support models, as well as to those that focus mainly on parenting programme delivery.

Many small-scale and some larger-scale studies are available which describe the work of individual family support services. While many of these services share characteristics and approaches, they do not equate to a generally and widely recognised 'model' as such. Having said that, there are services run by third-sector agencies which are delivered nationally, such as Action for Children's Family Partners and Quarriers Family Support Service in Scotland, the main features of which may be seen by those organisations as constituting a particular model. The Family Nurse Partnership Model, developed in the USA where it is known as the Nurse Family Partnership, and now in use across the UK, is another example of a model with specific characteristics (Olds, 2006; Barnes *et al.*, 2011). The programme is an evidence-based, nurse home-visiting programme . It is offered to first-time young mothers early in pregnancy (if possible, before seventeen-weeks gestation), continuing until their child is twenty-four months old. There are three main aims: to improve maternal and child pregnancy outcomes; to enhance child health and developmental outcomes; and to encourage parent's economic self-sufficiency. Families are visited weekly or fortnightly with specific materials used at each visit; standardised data forms record both the visits and details of the participants' progress (Barnes *et al.*, 2011).

Clearly, there are child and family support services that operate in particular settings, such as those that take place in schools, and some of these follow a definable model: for example, the Families and Schools Together (FAST) model (McDonald *et al.*, 2015). There are also support services that are provided with particular family circumstances in mind, such as those for parents who misuse drug and alcohol, although these share many of the characteristics of broader support services. In fact, it is probably more helpful to talk about the shared approaches which characterise many services rather than particular models. Some of those that have been identified by researchers in this field include:

- intervening early before problems become entrenched;
- giving a clear rationale for how the service will help;
- building on strengths as well as tackling weaknesses;
- taking time to understand the family's own perspective of their needs;
- building an empathic relationship, which is key to engagement by parents;
- recognising that some families will need long-term support (Statham and Biehal, 2005; Daniel and Rioch, 2007).

Many of these characteristics are endorsed by the parents whose views we have drawn on in this book.

While these principles are admirable ones to work towards, there are parents who, for various reasons, resist or undermine involvement by professionals to the extent to which it is not possible for their children to live safely at home. In this situation, some of the partnership aspects of working with them to provide support may not be possible (Davies and Ward, 2012). We discuss this in more detail throughout the book.

Who delivers family support? How do models vary accordingly?

There are many professionals delivering family support from across a range of disciplines. Some of these (e.g. health visitors) will approach the provision of support from their own particular practice background and be based on their specific training. In the case of health visitors, while their main focus will necessarily be on the health of the parent and child, they will be mindful of the family's practical and emotional needs. The emphasis on integrated, multi-agency working in the UK means that there should now be open channels for practitioners involved with a family to discuss with colleagues from other disciplines how other supports can be offered. The family would usually be aware of these discussions.

The role of local authority social workers in the UK in providing direct support to families is the subject of much discussion. Their work with families is underpinned by national frameworks such as GIRFEC in Scotland (Scottish Government, 2008), now enshrined in legislation, and UNO-CiNI (Northern Ireland Executive, 2011). In England and Wales, practice is based on the principles of the *Every Child Matters* strategy (Department of Health, 2003), with each local authority developing its own practice rather than following a national framework. Local authority social workers have a remit to assess the needs of families and, in some cases – particularly when statutory measures are required, to arrange, manage and contribute to the provision of supports. The extent to which they themselves provide family support would seem to depend on a number of factors including caseload, the availability of other family support services locally and individual team working practices.

Eileen Munro (2011), in her review of child protection, makes a plea for social workers to be enabled to prioritise direct contact with children and families over the increasing bureaucratic demands placed on them by managerial structures and procedures. Children and families told her they wanted to make positive relationships with social workers, and social workers themselves said they had entered the profession thinking this would be possible. Their professional training had gone some way towards equipping them with the necessary skills to do this, although some felt de-skilled by the lack of time and opportunity to work with families in a concerted and meaningful way, once they were employed.

Family support: evidence of effectiveness

There are a number of reviews that examine the evidence for different models of parenting support, particularly those that are centred around well-known and usually accredited parenting programmes such as Mellow Parenting and The Incredible Years (Moran *et al.*, 2004; Barrett, 2003). Studies have been done which look at the effectiveness of models such as the Family Nurse Partnership (Barnes *et al.*,

2011). However, there is a gap in studies about the effectiveness of different models of family support. This may be because it is less easily defined and has a much broader scope. Some studies undertaken by practitioners and academics do provide useful knowledge about the many forms of family support and their effectiveness (Quinton, 2004; Davies and Ward, 2012; Walker *et al.*, 2005). Recently, the evaluation of the Troubled Families Initiative has sought to measure the outcomes for families of that particular model (Day *et al.*, 2016). There are also numerous small-scale studies, which are mainly descriptive and focus on the process and approaches to family support employed by specific services. Increasingly, these do include some form of evaluation, usually using qualitative methods, although some employ a mixed-methods approach, with both qualitative and quantitative evidence included. Such evaluations are often used to try to assess the effectiveness of a service at a local level, and most are not widely published.

Although qualitative research, like quantitative, can vary in quality, its blanket dismissal as 'anecdotal and unscientific' is now rare (Moran *et al.*, 2004). In their review of parenting support, Moran *et al.* talk of the importance of process, as well as outcomes, in assessing the impact of delivering support programmes, and of what they call 'practice wisdom' – the learning from experienced practitioners, informed by many years of work in the field.

In their Supporting Families briefing in 2005, Statham and Biehal (2005) conclude that research studies that have tried to evaluate support services using quantifiable methods, such as standardised measures, are few and had generally been unable to demonstrate their effectiveness, beyond parents and families themselves finding them helpful. They acknowledge that this may be more to do with the challenges in evaluating such services in a meaningful way rather than the failings of services themselves.

There are some models of family support that have been or are currently being evaluated using what is considered to be a more rigorous approach. One example of a comprehensive evaluation is the ongoing one of Sure Start children's centres, which provide family support in England (Sammons *et al.*, 2015). A number of aspects of the work of staff in the centres is being investigated, including the impact on children and their families. Findings so far suggest that the support offered has had some degree of impact on what is described as family functioning and parenting outcomes.

Another model that is often cited as demonstrating effectiveness is that of the role of school nurses in Finland, in working with families whose children have been abused (Paavilainen *et al.*, 2000). The model used and the approach taken by nurses, categorised as active and firm or passive and uninvolved, are described, and conclusions are drawn about the effectiveness of the active and firm approach.

There is still work to be done in exploring the effectiveness of a resilience-based approach to family support work. Studies that have looked at the practice of a resilience-based approach to work with children found that it can be difficult to pin down the ways in which this differs from a more general strengths-based approach (Daniel *et al.*, 2009). This may well be the case with family resilience approaches, too. However, we do have some evidence that this approach can identify ways of working with families to help them develop greater resilience. In their evidence review of parenting and resilience, Hill *et al.* (2007), while acknowledging that there are gaps in this evidence, identify parental characteristics that are seen as helpful for parents and their children in developing resilience and coping with stress. These include open communication styles, problem-centred coping, flexibility and confidence.

In this book we do not advocate any particular model of family support as we believe that families may require different types and levels of support at different stages of their lives. Our aim is to reflect what parents told us was helpful to them, in the hope that this will be useful for practitioners in considering what form of family support they provide and how they approach it.

In order to really measure the effectiveness of family support for families and children in the longer term, longitudinal studies would be required. This might necessitate making contact with families who received support at some period(s) of their lives and who subsequently managed well without recourse to services other than universal ones. Tracking down research participants over long periods of time can be difficult, and this would require a well-resourced and comprehensive research study. In Chapter 6, we consider some ways in which the impact of family support can be measured, at least in the short term.

Family support: the political perspective

As in all areas of government-led social policy, there are political aspects to family support. On the face of it, all UK political parties agree about the desirability of children being safe and nurtured, and believe that families, on the whole, are the best people to provide for their children's care. However, at various times, policies are driven by particular 'moral panics', which grip the public's attention and are often the result of over-blown media stories (Cohen, 2002). Notions about good parenting are highly value-laden, and many subtle forms of pressure and control are imposed on parents to persuade them to conform to parenting norms, usually those valued by the middle class (Rose, 1989).

Government policies designed to support families often seem inco-herent and contradictory. For example, funding is put into expensive and intensive support for 'types' of families who are considered to be vulner-able (Olds, 2006) or disruptive to their communities (Day *et al.*, 2016), while, at the same time, the lives of these and many other families are made more difficult by punitive welfare benefits policies and lack of access to adequate housing. Cuts to local authority budgets mean that family sup-port provided by their own and by third-sector staff is increasingly reduced and rationed.

Political drivers also shape the operation of UK child protection sys-tems and family support services. There is a division between the highly proceduralised and formal child protection system and child welfare-pro-moting level of support provided to children and their families. These are described as the two orientations of child protection and family service (Stafford *et al.*, 2012). These effectively operate in parallel with two sepa-rate systems governing their practice, rather than the two being seen as integrated and part of a continuum of support. In general, the various child-related Acts across the UK have reinforced this separation by emphasising risks over needs once the family becomes involved with the child protec-tion system.

The GIRFEC framework in Scotland (Scottish Government, 2008) is designed to work across these systems in order to avoid this divide, and some areas are working hard to achieve this, but there are challenges associ-ated with it, given the risk-averse culture in which they function.

One of the consequences of this division is that, in some areas of the UK at least, the work of local authority social workers is limited to that which involves families whose children are in the child protection system or on statutory orders. The role of many is now focused primarily on case management and in preparing reports for the many meetings statutory and child protection work involves. Often the direct work of supporting families is undertaken by commissioned third-sector services (Munro, 2011). As well as frustrating for those social workers who joined the profession to work directly with people, this can lead to the divisive situation where families see social workers as enforcers and family support staff as being more friendly and 'on their side' (Buckley, 2005). If family support services are not available, families often feel that they are given insufficient guidance and help to enable them to care safely for their child and to be clear about what they need to do to exit the child protection system (Burgess and Stone, 2013).

For practitioners who have an interest in the political aspects of family support, parenting and child protection policy, there are several useful books that explore this subject in detail (Stafford *et al.*, 2012). Another thoughtful perspective on balancing state intervention with parental self-determination is that of Fox Harding (1997), who identifies four value positions in childcare policy: laissez faire and patriarchy; state paternalism and child protection; the modern defence of the birth family and parent's rights; and the more recent emphasis on children's rights.

Summary points

❏ A theory offers a systematic way of understanding a situation and a basis for why we think that undertaking family support in the way we do is likely to be effective.

❏ It is important to have a theoretical background to our work so that we can explain it to others; it gives us a structure to ensure that we stay on track in our work with families.

❏ Ecological theory is widely used as a basis for child and family support work and has been developed for use in assessment and planning for children and their families.

❏ Family resilience is a useful concept in thinking about how to help a family to sustain improvements made during a period of family support.

❏ While parenting support, particularly parenting programmes, have been described in numerous evaluations, models of family support are harder to pin down. We know more about general approaches to family support than we do about particular models, as these are so varied.

❑ There is a political aspect to family support, driven by notions of 'troubled' and 'troublesome' families. Policies to support families are often undermined by welfare benefits policies, which actually make life more difficult for them.

CHAPTER 2

Remembering the basics

'Some of us need help earlier on than we get it and the places we can go to for help need to be advertised, so we know about them.' Parent consultant, study F

Introduction

This chapter outlines the main ways in which practitioners become involved in providing family support, and the implications this may have for forming co-operative working relationships with parents. We then explore what parents told us about the importance of first meetings with practitioners, whether this is in their own home or at the premises of a 'helping' agency. We look at what parents said can help to make this initial meeting less threatening and more productive, and consequently more likely that they will accept the help being offered to them. Finally, we make some suggestions about how we can become better at 'reaching out' to parents so they feel more able to ask for help.

How do we become involved with families?

From our research and practice, we have identified three main ways in which practitioners become involved in supporting families. The initial reasons for services becoming involved, as well as the family's circumstances and past experiences, will influence the extent to which parents feel able to accept professional help. Practitioners will usually want to work 'in partnership' with families as far as possible; however, parents report that a number of factors can get in the way of this.

The main ways of becoming involved with services are when:

- parents actively ask for help;
- parents 'signal' their need for help;
- families are referred for help or support is 'offered' to them,

sometimes because professionals are worried that children's behaviour is masking distress or unhappiness.

We will consider what parents told us about how it feels to be at the receiving end of helping services when meeting practitioners for the first time, in relation to each of these three situations. Based on this, we will then offer ideas about how we can try to make this a better experience for them.

Parents actively seeking help

> 'It's a fine line between asking for help or not – will it look like I'm struggling? Will they think I'm struggling too much and take my bairns [children] away?' Parent, study G

It is not easy to admit to yourself or to others that you need help, although most of us have to do so from time to time. It is relatively easy to ask friends or family for assistance, especially if we can offer something in return, or if we are paying for the services of someone with specialist skills. It is much harder to admit that you are finding it hard to cope with caring for your children, and it is a big leap to ask for help with this from strangers. Although a whole industry has sprung up which is dedicated to parenting advice, to some extent the myth that parenting is instinctive still exists. Many of us learn how to parent our children in a safe and nurturing way from our family and friends, yet we know that many parents have not had this opportunity. Research studies have looked at the reasons why many of them are hesitant to seek help (Daniel *et al.*, 2011; Davies and Ward, 2012), and parents who talked to us said similar things, namely that:

- They are not sure who to go to:

> 'It is really difficult to get help, you go to somewhere and then you don't meet the criteria, but we don't know what the criteria are, no one ever tells us.' Parent, study G

- They think their problems are not bad enough and fear being turned away:

> 'It's hard to ask for help – they don't give it until they decide we need it.' Parent, study G

- They worry that it could lead to official interference in their lives and loss of control for themselves:

'Sometimes you wish you'd never asked for help because everything you do is put under the spotlight.' Parent consultant, study F

Parents told us that they had to swallow their pride and summon up considerable courage to approach services, as they were often unsure about what sort of response they would get. That is why some said they were more likely to talk to their GP, health visitor (if they had one) or a familiar teacher or helper at their child's school, particularly if the school had an open door policy on offering parental support.

On the face of it, we might think that providing help and advice would be fairly straightforward when parents have sought it out. In some cases it is, and there will be clear ways in which we can provide the help required or identify another agency that could.

However, even when they have taken that leap to ask for help from their GP or health visitor, some parents told us that they had to be very persistent or shown signs of desperation in order to get a response:

'It took ages for me to be allocated a health visitor – I had to cry on the phone before one finally came out. You have to be at breaking point before you can get help.' Parent, study H

We are not good at 'opening doors' to those who need help (Daniel *et al.*, 2011) and we will look at ways in which we could improve this later in the chapter.

Parents told us that it feels easier to say that you need help with something small or practical than admitting, even to yourself, that you are not coping with the demands of being a parent, whatever the reasons might be for that. Parenting in itself is a hard task, but if you are doing so while trying to cope with depression, perhaps coupled with financial or other pressures, it can be unmanageable. Many parents have deep-seated problems which, not surprisingly, they initially feel unable to talk about. Parents said they often feel overwhelmed by a mix of practical and emotional problems, and it will take quite a while before they can explain this or open up about them to a stranger:

'They supported me to get my house and helped me decorate it. They gave me advice about parenting an under-five year old. Eventually I told them about why I was struggling. I don't like to actually ask for help or advice as that feels like failure but my support worker offers it so that helps.' Parent, study J

Some parents initially describe their child's behaviour as the reason why they find it hard to parent them. And, of course, it may well be one of the reasons for them needing help, as children are likely to be reacting to the way their parents are looking after them. The best starting point for practitioners working in family support can be to try to form an understanding of the situation as parents see it. From there, it may be possible to explain to them the reasons why children may be acting as they are.

In some cases, what parents tell practitioners they need help with, and what help the practitioner thinks they need, may be two very different things. Or there may be truth in both points of view. In any case, it is necessary to build a relationship which enables problems to be unpicked, a shared understanding to develop and negotiation to take place about what needs to be done. This can take time but, if approached sensitively, may lead to parents feeling able to talk about any deep-seated problems in their lives which are influencing the care of their children.

Parents also told us that asking for help for themselves can be seen by practitioners as not putting their children's needs above their own:

'It's hard for us to know where to go for help when things start to get difficult. Sometimes we ask for help for ourselves so we can look after our children better but this is sometimes taken the wrong way and people think that we are putting ourselves first.' Parent consultant, study F

Some parents felt that it was hard to ask for help in the 'right' way or in a way that would not be misunderstood. The perception of some was that they only got support when social workers thought it was time – that this was rationed and was only available to those who were on the point of not being able to cope. It is, indeed, the case that services are generally provided on the basis of availability rather than need (Vincent, 2015).

Reflective exercise

We all need to ask for help from time to time. Think about an occasion when you had to ask for help from a stranger or for something you felt uncomfortable or embarrassed about? How did it feel – both before you asked and while you were doing it? What might have made it easier for you?

Parents 'signalling' their need for help

'I wish other mums could hear about this service, maybe through their GP. Lots of mums keep quiet about their mental health problems and feel ashamed. Sometimes it has to come out in other ways. If I didn't speak out and talk to someone in the first place I would never have had this help. You can overcome your illness.' Parent, study H

Directly asking for help can sometimes be too difficult, and parents who are in contact with universal services may show their need for support by their actions rather than by asking for it. It is up to professionals to be on the alert for signs from parents, as well as from children, that help may be needed. A careful approach is required in responding to these signs, so that parents are not put off taking up support or being directed elsewhere for it. Staff in universal services who build a trusting relationship with families can be a good bridge to parents feeling confident enough to place their trust in targeted support services. There is some evidence that this is taking place in the operation of GIRFEC in Scotland (Kosonen, 2011):

'Some teachers listen to us, are available when we need them and understand things, like when the children are late for school. Some have stuck by us and they can pick up on things and ring social workers for us when we need help.' Parent consultant, study F

When help is 'offered' to parents

We didn't like it when we got a letter saying make sure your daughter will be present at home when we come, we thought they were going to take her away. They didn't ring us – they just wrote and turned up–it would be easier for us if they had rung.' Parent, study G

In some situations, families may be visited by local authority social workers or health professionals because someone has worries about the care of the children and whether parents are coping. Unless health visitors stay involved with them because of identified difficulties, some families have little or no contact with services when children are very young, and problems may be picked up only later on, when children's behaviour at nursery or school gives cause for professionals to worry about them.

Once possible difficulties are picked up, families can be referred to targeted services and, while parents will usually be aware that a referral has been made and may have been asked to agree to it, this is not always the case. In many instances, parents may not think that they need help and may see contact with professionals as interference. It is not hard to imagine how the prospect of a visit by someone in authority, or who has been called in by a statutory agency, can lead to parents feeling anxious and defensive. They are often unsure of the position or role of professionals who come to their home or who they meet at the offices of a service, and they may feel they have little power in the situation.

Some parents have had past experiences of involvement with social work services, which they found difficult or led to major changes in their lives: for example, being removed from their birth families (Shemmings and Shemmings, 2001). It is no wonder that some parents feel, and act, defensively and come across as wary or hostile. This can be particularly hard for those with difficult early life experiences, such as growing up in a family where they felt they had little personal control or where the culture was to challenge those in authority.

Parents told us that, at the very least, they felt anxious that their lives and actions would be assessed and judged, and that they would be found wanting. If family relationships are strained and the house is disorganised, parents may be aware that the first impression that professionals get when coming to their home will not be good. Parents sometimes described how they had become used to daily life feeling out of control and expected nothing different; some did not know where to turn for help or lacked the confidence to talk to anyone who might be able to assist them.

Family example: Chris

Chris was a young father caring for his son, Gavin, aged two. He was estranged from his family, and Gavin's mother had little contact with him. Chris' GP had referred him to social services after he attended the surgery and talked about feeling depressed and unable to cope. A support worker from the local early intervention service rang to say she would come to see him. Chris had been accommodated for a short spell as a child and, although he had returned home, he was worried about becoming involved with social workers. He was very anxious about the visit, and the flat was spotless when the support worker arrived. Chris was very defensive about his situation at first but, after much reassurance by the support worker, became more open to the idea of accepting help, initially to meet other fathers and give Gavin opportunities to meet other children and adults.

One of the most important messages from parents was:

> 'First of all, try to put yourselves in our shoes. It's hard when you feel that your life is not your own and that you have no control over what happens to you and your children.' Parent consultant, study F

We cannot emphasise enough how important it is to consciously try to do this – even though the family's experiences may seem very alien to our own. It can be instructive if practitioners are able to imagine reversing roles with parents, understand their situation and feel what it would be like to live with the pressures some of them are facing every day:

> 'We always imagine that you professionals have a perfect life where nothing ever goes wrong.' Parent consultant, study F

First meetings: A crucial time

> 'The first impression we get when we meet you is very important. Whether you speak to us clearly and respectfully and whether you show an interest in us and our children as individuals. We would like you to listen to us and talk with us rather than at us.' Parent consultant, study F

Parents talked in detail about their first contact with a professional. It was important to them that practitioners set a tone that made parents feel respected and listened to and which showed a genuine interest in both them and their children. The atmosphere of this first meeting, and how it goes, may be influenced by where the discussion is taking place and what 'props' we have to hand to try to make it as reassuring and relaxed as possible for parents, given what may well be stressful circumstances for them.

Practitioners' perspectives

Practitioners are usually coping with workload pressures; they may have little time to reflect on their role and think clearly about what they are trying to achieve when they meet the family. They may become caught up in following procedures and fulfilling the demands of bureaucracy, and this can affect their ability to relate to parents (Munro, 2011). If they are clear in their own minds, they are more likely to be clear with parents about their purpose in meeting them. Are they aiming to find out and assess what support is needed, with a view to providing it, or some of it, themselves? Or to identify other services that might? Or is there another purpose and can this be explained clearly? When a practitioner first meets a family, there may be a number of things that have a bearing on how they 'tune in' to them, and this, in turn, will influence how the family responds. These things could include:

- preconceived ideas that the practitioner may have about the family, taken from referral notes or conversations with staff from their own or other agencies;
- a preoccupation with the visit or meeting the practitioner just came from or one due to happen later in the day;
- shortage of time, if the workload means they are trying to fit too much into the day;
- the demands of the practitioner's agency: for example, to make a quick initial assessment of the family's situation and needs;
- how the practitioner responds to hostility, unresponsiveness or, at the other extreme, being bombarded with problems, perhaps emotional and practical, which may feel overwhelming. On the one hand, they need to be prepared to respond to what may be a distressing physical environment and emotional life stories. On the other hand, they may be met with a family who are unwilling to communicate at all.
- Some of these are part and parcel of the working day, but it can be helpful to be aware of them, go in with an open mind and have strategies for dealing with them.

Environment: Meeting families outside the home

> 'If I go through that door, go looking for help, will I be accused of harming my children? Or will they (services) get involved for a while and then walk out of the door again.' Parent, study G

Many parents told us how hard it was for them to go into the office of a 'helping' service because of their anxieties about meeting strangers and lack of confidence in new situations. This added to their feelings of inadequacy about seeking help in the first place. If practical, some parents had found it helpful to go along with a health visitor or someone they knew.

It does not help that many social work and health service waiting and meeting rooms are not welcoming places – many reception staff are seated behind security glass, and waiting rooms are full of posters about drug use and health problems. Some social work offices are no longer in local communities, and this can make it harder for parents to travel to and approach them. It is the opposite of what we know families value – neighbourhood-based support services (Holman *et al.*, 1999). Even some children's or family centres run by third-sector agencies have security entrances, and parents said they missed the open style of family centres, where they felt more able to just 'drop in':

> 'Our family centre used to be in a flat up the road and then you could just walk in, but now you have to be referred. It's still good but it was better when you could just decide to come in. If you called in just for advice they wouldn't turn you away.'
> Parent, study G

The entrance can send a strong message to parents about their impoverished situation and their feelings of, and even seemingly small things such as improving signage and the wording of such signs can make a difference.

We understand that it may not be practical to improve 'corporate' entrances, which may be used for several different services. However, there may be alternative premises that can be used to meet families. Schools and nurseries usually make efforts to be welcoming (although most have some form of security entrance now), and some have family rooms which can be booked. Health centres may be another option, if there are private spaces available, and these usually have the advantage of being within local communities.

Even buildings that are bleak and daunting on the outside can provide a welcoming space on the inside, with a room transformed by some imagination, comfy chairs and relaxing colours.

Case example: a Family Support Service in Glasgow

This service, run by a third-sector agency was housed in an old, run-down school building, which many local parents were reluctant to enter because of their negative memories of their school days there. It was half empty, and the staff, employed by the building owners, who worked at the secure entrance did not even greet those who came in. Once inside the family support service rooms, the atmosphere was bright, welcoming and friendly. The service admin worker welcomed families into the office, where staff always stopped what they were doing to talk with them. Well-decorated parents' and children's rooms made them feel relaxed and valued; tea and toast were provided and enjoyed. It felt to parents like a haven from the harshness of the local environment.

Environment: Home visits

> 'It would help to have a better explanation of why social workers have come and what could be done to help. They have so much power – could they not be just a little more friendly?' Parent, study G

Just as many parents told us of their anxieties about meeting practitioners at an office, others told us that it can be equally difficult for them when one comes to their home. Wherever this first meeting takes place, most of them felt that they were being judged, and this caused some to react in a number of ways, which included being defensive or hostile.

It can also be difficult as a practitioner to enter a family home and meet the parents for the first time (Ferguson, 2010). In addition to being conscious of parents' anxiety and possibly hostility, practitioners may be feeling apprehensive about what they will find in the home and about having potentially difficult exchanges, especially if parents feel that their care of their children is being questioned. Of course, the practitioner may not even get an answer at the door or be allowed over the doorstep. Persistence is important. It may be necessary for practitioners to leave notes, shout through the letterbox (in an encouraging and friendly way, of course) and make it clear that they will not be put off:

> 'I hated the staff coming round at first, I felt as if they were coming to interfere. I spoke to my health visitor who said I should give it a try. I wouldn't answer the door but staff would

stay till they got an answer, they were like a dog with a bone – never giving up. But I started seeing how my life could be, that was the first time I realised what I was doing to my health to my wee boy and my baby.' Parent, study D

Once in the house, there may be situational distractions to deal with, such as a loud television, visitors, hostile partners, dogs and mobile phones. Practitioners have to observe and take in all that is going on, as well as hold a conversation. If children are present, they will need to form an initial impression of how safe and well they are. Ways can usually be found to interest the child so that there is some conversation or other interaction with them.

The main aim of the first meeting will probably be for the practitioner to give a clear explanation of who they are and why they are there – a discussion that shows a genuine interest in parents and their children is also helpful. The way that a practitioner words things is also important – most parents want the best for their children and, unless there are clear signs to the contrary, if the practitioner can say 'we know that you want the best for your child' and 'we want to help you with that' a positive starting point and shared aim might be created.

That said, practitioners need to be open and honest with parents and say that, if they are worried that the child is not safe, they will need to talk to other professionals. This ongoing assessment of risk must be in their minds from the first meeting with the family, during any subsequent 'assessment' period and beyond. Parents do realise this – and some clearly said that they preferred practitioners to be open about this from the start:

> 'It's hard for social workers – they have to be suspicious because some parents are abusive, so they need to be vigilant. Some parents are very clever at covering things up and talk a good game. The social workers have to look at the child's welfare and ask the right questions.' Parent, study G

Practitioners also need to be sensitive to relationship pressures, perhaps from a partner or other person, present or not, who is dismissive or negative about support services. Practitioners may need to find a way to meet the primary parent at another venue and, if possible, without this other person present. This does not mean that important people in a child's life should be excluded – their role in the family does need to be explored at some point.

Key points: what parents tell us makes meeting professionals easier

Wherever the first meeting takes place, whether at their home or at a service's premises, parents told us that the following made a crucial difference to them:

○ **Time**: It was important to parents that the practitioner set aside sufficient time to have a relaxed discussion about what was going on with the family and did not rush in late and watch the clock after half an hour; this was considered particularly important for the first meeting:

> **'It's best when people can spend time with us and are not rushing off – that makes us feel like we're just a statistic and another thing on the 'to-do' list, that it's just about filling in the paperwork.' Parent, study G**

○ **Listening**: Parents were very attuned to the extent to which they thought that practitioners really listened to them; the first meeting was seen as a time when some parents felt the need to offload, even if it was not always about what practitioners had come to discuss:

> **'They need to listen – do they really hear that you want help? Sometimes it feels like they are "on a different roundabout".' Parent, study G**

○ **Language**: Parents disliked the use of jargon and wanted clear explanations about who practitioners were, why they were meeting them and what they might be able to do to help:

> **'We need clear information and advice and we need you to use language that makes sense to us.' Parent consultant, study F**

○ **No paperwork**: Parents told us how much they disliked practitioners appearing with a clipboard and a form of pre-set questions and that, at this first meeting, an informal discussion was helpful. Talking with someone who is scribbling away was described as very off-putting; a 'to-do' list in a notebook at the end was fine and reassured them that they had been listened to:

> **'She came out and listened the first time – without any paperwork or anything – I just offloaded and she didn't judge. She treats us with respect and is easy to talk to.' Parent, study J**

○ **Finding common ground**: Parents found it helpful if a practical action could be mutually agreed at the end of the first visit, so that they could see that some concrete support was available and that being involved with services could make a difference, even if this was a small one to start with. However, making false promises or not completing this action, were not helpful for future relationships:

'They do need to follow through. You can get that you don't trust people to do what they say they will so it's good when they come back and say that even a little thing has happened for the better.' Parent, study E

○ **Including fathers, particularly if present**: Mothers and fathers alike told us that they often felt that questions about parenting were addressed primarily to mothers. In many families, fathers and male carers take an active role in their children's upbringing, and it was appreciated if this was acknowledged and they were included:

'Society is not set up for men looking after kids. It's not set up for both parties to have an equal role with both having control.' Parent, study P

Including the children

It is important that practitioners meet the children and young people in the family at the earliest opportunity. In the first instance, this will probably take place with parents present, but it may be important to spend time with children away from their parents, perhaps at school or somewhere that feels safe for them. As we mentioned in the Introduction, there are numerous books and practice guides about talking with and involving children in assessment and ongoing support, and it is not our purpose to cover this in our book.

The bigger picture: Reaching out to parents

'Services need to be more accessible. Sometimes it's really hard to track them down.' Parent, study G

We know that some parents are unlikely to approach social work services for help, given their fears about official interference and that their children will be removed. So how can we reach out to them and make it acceptable to ask for help? At an organisational level, there are things that could be done and which practitioners can try to influence. The suggestions from parents included:

- leaflets in health centres or information on the Internet so that they can avoid asking GPs and others for help directly;
- more frequent and longer visits from health visitors would be welcomed by many parents, as long as a good relationship had been made with them;
- a parent support worker, or social worker, based in nurseries and

schools, so that they are a familiar face before parents approach them. Parents felt that nurseries, in particular, were places which most parents attended and staff there could, resources permitted, provide support without the shame or stigma attached to going into a targeted service; schools were often more difficult places to seek help unless parents' groups and meeting places were provided for this purpose on school premises;

- family and children's centres were seen by some parents as acceptable places to go, especially if they could 'drop in' rather than being referred. Even so, some were anxious about going into them, so having a health visitor or someone else they knew going with them for the first few visits was seen as helpful:

> 'It's a big step to go to a family centre and join a group – my health visitor took me to Sure Start – she put her arm round my shoulder to get me through that door.' Parent, study G

Key points: removing barriers

This could be done by:
- ○ providing services which parents can walk to within their local communities;
- ○ providing support workers in settings that parents felt did not 'show them up' (e.g. health centres, nurseries and schools);
- ○ making services open to parents passing by (not having to be buzzed in, at least from the street);
- ○ ensuring that very anxious parents have someone to 'hold their hand' until they get used to going along to support services.

Reflecting on what has taken place at this first stage

So, the first meeting with the family has taken place, and time is needed to think about what should happen next to support the family to care for their child.

Considerations could include:
- How the first meeting went: how do I, as the practitioner, feel about it and how might the parents feel now?
- Is the child safe in the immediate future? If not, who do I consult?
- Have I been open and honest with parents that my priority is for

children to be safe and that I will talk to other professionals at any stage if I am worried that they are not?

- If the child is safe, what is my initial impression of what support might be needed? Am I (or is my agency) the person to provide it?
- If further assessment is required – what is the priority within this and how shall I approach it? Is it best done in the family home or are there alternative places?
- Are there practical tasks that I agreed to follow up for the family?

If possible, it is usually helpful for the practitioner to talk some of this over with a colleague, particularly if there are areas of worry or doubt.

If the decision is that the family does not require support, any initial help agreed with the family should be arranged and the practitioner should contact the parents to explain why they will not be visiting again, at least for the time being. The door should always be left open for parents to contact the agency or another one that could help them, if necessary, and preferably with a named contact person provided.

If an assessment is required, read on ... this is discussed in the next chapter.

Summary points

- ❏ Parents told us that asking for, and sometimes accepting, help is difficult; they gave us ideas about some ways in which services could reach out to them and make it easier for them to receive the support they need in a way that avoided them feeling that they might lose all power in the situation.

- ❏ There are tensions for parents and practitioners when help is imposed, rather than sought. Parents appreciate practitioners showing sensitivity in this situation, being empathic and also clear about the reasons for their involvement.

- ❏ The first meeting between parent and practitioner is important in setting the tone for future relationships; parents valued practitioners who listened as well as being clear about how they might be able to help.

- ❏ Practitioners' visits to the family home can be difficult for both parents and practitioners to manage. Parents say they usually feel judged, and practitioners can help alleviate parents' anxieties if they find common ground with the parent, primarily about the best interests of the children.

❏ Entering an office or the premises of a 'helping' service can be daunting for families. Practitioners can ask parents what might make this easier for them, and try to ensure that this support is in place – particularly at the start.

CHAPTER 3

The art of assessment

'I did a form which said what my aims were and it was good to be involved in deciding what I needed help with – although other things did crop up. I also did a 'My World' assessment about my child and found it easy to understand.' Parent, study H

Introduction

The next crucial step in the practitioner's involvement with the family is for them to assess the child's safety and well-being, as well as any support the family requires to ensure this. In this chapter, we look at why assessment is important and what parents told us being assessed feels like to them. We explore what practitioners themselves may bring to the assessment. We refer to some of the assessment frameworks that practitioners use, and what parents told us about using visual and other creative materials to help make their involvement in the assessment more meaningful. We outline a possible structure for assessment, and the visual tools that might be used as part of this.

Our focus in this chapter is on what parents told us about the assessment of their parenting and what they contributed to the assessment of their child. It is clearly important that children are also involved in the assessment of their development and care needs and, while we do not cover that in this book, we suggest some of the many books and practice guides that offer creative ways to involve them.

Why do we assess families?
Having met the family, finding out in more detail what daily life is like for them is the next step towards drawing up a plan of support with them and thinking about who might best provide any support required. This assessment plays a part in enabling practitioners to find out if children

are safe and well, which must always be their main aim. If parents are finding it hard to provide nurturing care for their children, practitioners need to try to discover what is preventing them from doing so and what is influencing the way in which they are looking after them. The act of doing this with the family, if undertaken carefully, can help practitioners start to form a co-operative relationship with parents and children. It may help practitioners to work together with parents to see what could be put in place to make daily life less stressful and more satisfying for themselves, and safer and more nurturing for their children.

Practitioners also need to know how things are at the start of their work with the family so that there is a 'baseline' against which the usefulness of the support can be measured.

The word 'assessment'
Parents told us that the word 'assessment' can be off-putting. Rather than seeing it as an assessment of their support needs, with the potential of being helpful to them and their children, they said that it felt like a long period of intrusive questioning designed to find out if they were a good parent or not. They told us that they felt they had to prove themselves and were not sure what to do to 'pass the test'. Some parents explained that they had been the subject of many assessments and that these had not always led to support being put in place to try to make things better for them – in fact, it felt as though little changed as a result. Some of the questions made little sense to them. Parents described the assessment process as 'having to answer the same old questions' or 'telling our story over and over again to different people':

> 'If you ask for help and say you can't cope, you have to keep going through your story – services aren't good at passing information on.' Parent, study G

Practitioners and researchers have identified what is known as 'assessment paralysis' (Reder and Lucey, 1995). This is when continual re-assessments get in the way of planning and action to help the family. This may be due to a family's circumstances changing, a new worker becoming involved or because the family is being passed on to another agency. While families' circumstances do change and paperwork will need updating regularly, this should not mean that any help required is put on hold.

Parents also identified the danger of some assessments (whether a child, family or parenting one) becoming the end product in itself. In some cases, it appears that, once the assessment is completed, a decision is made that (a) leads to the family becoming part of a formal system, which involves many meetings but sometimes does not include the support needed to help the family move on from that system, or (b) denies the family support because the parents' care of the children is seen as acceptable and not 'bad enough' to warrant help. Parents talked to us about their frustrations when this happens:

> 'We need help before we have a crisis.' Parent consultant, study F

Some research suggests that assessment has become overly complicated and a source of anxiety for the practitioners who do the assessing, as well as for the families they are assessing (Daniel *et al.*, 2011). Standardised assessment forms with tight timescales for completion are seen by some social workers as meeting the bureaucratic needs of agencies rather than those of families. And some parents have also clearly picked up on this:

> 'Sometimes it just feels like a tick-box exercise and you lose interest.' Parent consultant, study F

It can be a very difficult process for those involved. This includes the practitioner who has to prioritise the needs of the child while being mindful of those of the parents, and has to offer support to try to prevent future difficulties, while not intervening unnecessarily and bearing in mind limited and rationed resources.

Reflective exercise

We are all assessed from time to time: for example, in job interviews and work appraisals. How does this make you feel, particularly if there is a lot at stake? How do you think you might feel if your parenting (or your role as a partner, sibling, daughter/son) was being assessed?

Fathers

> 'Social workers often leave dads out of things; it just doesn't seem to occur to them that dads can be important. They just

listened to what my partner had to say about me, without asking me.' Parent, study G

Although we have talked about parents in a way that assumes that we are including both mothers and fathers (or male and female carers), we must remember that fathers and male carers often feel overlooked when it comes to their inclusion in family assessments and the supports that are subsequently put in place. Many fathers play an important part in children's lives and, for many, they provide the most significant care. Even if they are living away from their child, the care they provide when they see him or her will have a bearing on the child's welfare. Practitioners need to ensure that the role of the child's father (and other male carers such as a stepfather) is assessed, and the potential strengths and risks of the relationship explored. We know that fathers can pose a danger to children, in physical and emotional ways (Family Rights Group, 2011). Practitioners' assessments may also entail trying to disentangle and make sense of conflicting accounts between parents, if relationships are difficult (Daniel and Taylor, 2005).

Family example: Bill and Lorraine

Bill and Lorraine were separated but had an on/off relationship, with Bill returning now and then to the family home, sometimes for several weeks at a time. Their son, Mark, aged seven, often stayed with him at his flat during breaks in Bill's relationship with Lorraine. It was difficult for the practitioner to pin him down to being part of the parenting assessment, as the relationship was 'on a break'. He enlisted the help of Bill's mother, who persuaded Bill to meet him. There were conflicting accounts between Bill and Lorraine about who provided the 'best' care for Mark, and the practitioner gathered the views of a number of other people, including Mark, in order to piece together a full picture of Mark's care. Bill and Lorraine did not agree with the completed assessment report, and their comments were included with it.

Being open and clear

'Sometimes the language used is hard to understand – the words are too long – so people need to slow it down. We can be scared to say we don't understand but my worker can usually tell by my face that I don't.' Parent, study L

Practitioners clearly need to be honest with parents about why they are asking such detailed questions and producing a written report of their family for other professionals to read. And while we know that some parents find the word 'assessment' intimidating, it is not easy to find an alternative word for it. It is usually on the forms that practitioners complete at the end of the process and which parents will see; practitioners should, of course, be open and up front about it. However, practitioners can describe and do the assessment in a way that helps parents see it as a shared, interesting and hopefully even 'empowering' activity. The benefits of an empowering approach to assessment are described by Thoburn *et al.* (1995), later quoted by Yvonne and David Shemmings in Horwath (2001):

- It leads to better safeguarding of the child's welfare.
- It recognises that family members possess unique knowledge about their own and each other's strengths and weaknesses.
- It acknowledges explicitly the rights of family members, which helps develop trust.

In their own work, Yvonne and David Shemmings (1996) describe the importance that parents place on professionals' honesty, answerability, sensitivity and even-handedness in working with them. They describe the use of guided conversations, rather than set questions, during the assessment process, which they describe as an important time when relationships with families are still being formed.

Practitioners should remind themselves that the parents they work with have differing levels of understanding and that it cannot be assumed that they always know what practitioners are talking about. Constant checking with parents that they do understand, and finding other ways to say it, may be required – it is up to practitioners to clarify what they are asking. There may be health and development factors that influence parents' ability to concentrate on and comprehend what is being said – there may also be emotional reasons why some of the conversations practitioners have with them just do not sink in. In all discussions that practitioners have with them, opportunities can be found to check if parents know what children need from them at different ages and stages – it should not be assumed that they do. In addition, we advocate, if at all possible, using methods which are visual, interactive and make sense to all those involved, some of which we will describe later in this chapter.

Practitioners also need to be open about the fact that they will be asking for information from other agencies, such as health services and schools, and adding some of this into the assessment report. This may be from written records or through talking to other professionals involved with the family. The idea of 'multi-agency' assessments is now common practice among professionals, but may be an alarming one for parents whose family information is being shared. Practitioners need to do what they can to reassure parents that they want to get a full picture of how things are for their family from the main people they have contact with, but that their views as parents are equally important.

Frameworks, approaches and models

Most practitioners now use one of a number of frameworks to structure their assessment of the child's needs and whether these are being met, and also to help them understand what is happening with the family. The assessment of the child is usually based around an ecological model, where the needs and risks of the child are assessed in relation to what is being provided by parents, or other primary carers, by the extended family and/or friends and by the wider community including schools and other services. This is likely to include a consideration of the risk and protective factors in the child's life and may use a resilience-based framework.

The GIRFEC framework used in Scotland, which includes the My World Triangle format, adopts this resilience-based approach (Scottish Government, 2012). The aim is to identify the positives in the child's support network, and to build on this, while minimising any risks to their safety and health. Chapter 1 included more detail, including references, about the theoretical bases of ecological and resilience-based frameworks and their development into practice tools for assessment, support planning and review.

There are other assessment frameworks which have been adopted by many services within the UK and wider, including the Graded Care Profile (Svrivastava et al., 2003) and Signs of Safety (Turnell and Edwards, 1999). These are used most often in child protection work, especially in relation to neglect. Signs of Safety makes use of creative visual tools, mainly for use with children but also some which may be helpful when assessing adults' care of children.

Parenting assessments often take place alongside the one which is concerned primarily with the child's needs. These aim to produce evidence about what is described as the 'quality' of parenting and/or parenting 'capacity'. *The Framework for Assessment of Children in Need and Their Families in England and Wales* (Department of Health, 2000) divides this into six parenting dimensions or activities which are necessary to keep a child safe, nurtured, healthy and stimulated. A way of thinking about parenting styles, and the possible effect of each on children, was devised by Baumrind (1972). These styles are categorised as authoritative, authoritarian, indulgent and indifferent, and they offer practitioners a way of assessing the impact of parenting and what changes might be made.

The openness and ability of parents to accept support to change the ways in which they care for their children is usually assessed as part of this or through the use of a separate form, which looks at this in more detail. These are commonly known as 'parental motivation' or 'capacity to change' assessments. The framework developed by Reder and Lucey (1995) is helpful, in that its categories include questions for practitioners to explore with parents about influences on their parenting, their attitudes to it, their relationships with their children and their potential for change, including their response to any previous interventions.

When looking at parents' willingness and ability to change, the model suggested by Horwath and Morrison (2001) is a useful one. It has two levels – those of effort and commitment – which are combined to suggest four possible categories: (a) genuine commitment; (b) tokenism; (c) compliance imitation, where commitment is not sustained; and (d) dissent or avoidance (low commitment and effort). While it can take some time to fully assess parents' ability to change, it is also important not to take too long or to give parents too many chances, when change appears unlikely (Brandon *et al.*, 2008).

For more ways of assessing parents' motivation, there are useful sections in Horwath (2013) and Taylor and Daniel (2005), both of which look at this in relation to child neglect. More recently, Platt *et al.* (2016) have developed a 'parental capacity to change' model or tool, known as C-Change, to help with this assessment; there is also a version that ties in with GIRFEC in Scotland.

Taken together, the information gathered in these assessments should enable a plan to be formed which aims to ensure that the child is looked after in a safe, healthy and nurturing way. If possible, this should include how parents can be supported to care for their child. However, the assessment may, of course, provide evidence that concludes that the parents are unlikely to manage this even with supports and that the child needs alternative family care.

The assessment formats mentioned above are widely used and well regarded; they are described in numerous practice guides and books, most of which also outline the theories on which they are based (Horwath, 2001; Davies and Ward, 2012). We will not outline them in detail here, given that the main focus of this chapter is to describe what parents found helpful in enabling them to make sense of, and feel active in, the assessment process, primarily that which looked at their parenting support needs.

A helpful starting point?

> 'We were given options about the type of support we could have and we said what we most needed help with, so we didn't have it imposed on us. The decisions I made were for me and my family.' Parent, study H

Parents told us that they appreciated it when practitioners began the parenting assessment by asking them what they thought they needed help with. They felt it made more sense to them if practitioners started from where they were and, even if they were unclear about this themselves, the discussion about this could be helpful. In some cases, these were small practical things, such as ideas about what could help with early morning, getting-ready-for-school routines or at bedtime, when they found it hard to get the children ready or settled. The 'Our Day' clock described later in this chapter as one of the assessment session tools can be a helpful way of starting a discussion about this.

ASSESSMENT SESSION EXERCISE

- Which times of the day are hardest? (looking at the 'Our day' clock, when are the stressful times?)
- Why is that? What is happening?
- What could make it better?

Parents liked the idea of setting practical and acheivable aims, even during the assessment, which might involve them trying out an idea with help from the practitioner (or another support worker) or the practitioner undertaking a task on their behalf. This allowed them to gain confidence (a) in the practitioner – that they genuinely wanted to help and/or (b) in themselves – that changes were possible, particularly in something that they themselves had decided was important to them. Practitioners reported that starting the relationship (and assessment) on this basis helped paved the way for more 'challenging' discussions, which might be required further down the line.

What do practitioners bring to the assessment?

Just as parents might bring their previous experiences of 'assessment' to the process, practitioners who do the assessment come to it with their own values, standards and personal experiences, which colour their views about 'good enough' parenting. Research explores the range of standards of what acceptable childcare looks like between staff working in different professions: for example, social workers compared with teachers; and between professionals working in helping services and those of the general public (Daniel *et al.*, 2011). Even those working within the same organisation may have different ideas about this (Horwath, 2005). There is some evidence that different standards may apply depending on the family's socio-economic group. Horwath discusses this in relation to the press coverage and the public's reactions to two cases of lack of parental supervision, which resulted in the disappearance of Madeleine McCann and the murder of Scarlett Keeling (Horwath, 2013). Madeleine, aged three, disappeared from her bed while on a family holiday, her parents having left her and her two younger siblings while they ate supper nearby, checking them every half hour. Scarlett, who was fifteen years old, was left in Goa with a twenty-five-year-old, male travel guide while her mother travelled on for a few days with the rest of the family – Scarlett was raped and murdered. While the UK tabloid press described the parents of both girls as 'middle class', their condemnation of Scarlett's mother, as an 'ageing hippie' with an 'alternative lifestyle', was far greater than that of Madeleine's parents, who were seen as respectable doctors. News coverage of Madeleine's disappearance was generally supportive of her parents.

ASSESSMENT CONSIDERATIONS

In undertaking an assessment, practitioners are balancing a number of things:

○ the welfare of the child, which is clearly the priority, while also having empathy for the difficulties that some parents may be facing;

○ the need to keep an open mind and avoid a situation where an initial impression is formed, and the evidence then found to back this up (Milner and O'Byrne, 2002);

○ the ability to make a judgement without being judgemental and paying selective attention to certain aspects of care (Milner and O'Byrne, 2002);

○ seeing the family and child in their own right and not making comparisons with the family the practitioner met earlier, whose needs were even greater;

○ weighing up the impact of parenting on this particular child (Cleaver, 2001); there may be some aspects of the care they receive which compensate for others that are missing.

Managing all this is a skilled task for the practitioner and requires personal and intellectual skills. The chance to learn from, and be supported by, other practitioners can be invaluable in helping less-experienced staff increase their skills in this area.

What should be included in the parenting assessment?

As we mentioned earlier, parents' views about the type of help they need are often a good starting point, and they are also likely to be part of the ongoing support planning. However, as the welfare of the child must be the overriding focus, the assessment process is primarily to help practitioners decide if the child's needs are being met. It may be that parents are not aware of all the needs that children have at different ages – their expectations of what the child can manage may be too high. Or it could be that they are unable to meet the child's needs at that particular time and, once practitioners know the reasons for this, they might be able to help them to do so:

> 'The assessment showed that I needed practical advice about how to cope with parenting our boys when my husband is away and I'm tired and not coping. I didn't have a good upbringing myself and I could see things were wrong but didn't know how to do it right and also kept forgetting how to put it into practice.'
> Parent, study H

The assessment must conclude with a plan about what, if any, supports are required to enable parents to care for their child. Practitioners may think that the parents will struggle to do this, even if intensive and long-term help can be provided by all available support networks, but evidence is required to back this up. If practitioners are to be as sure as possible that parents can care for their child, or can do so with support, information needs to be included that:

- assures practitioners that the child is sufficiently safe and healthy. Whenever they spend time with the family, practitioners need to consider what the risks might be for the child. If the child is clearly unsafe, immediate action will be required to take the steps needed to ensure that they are living with someone who will protect them;
- helps practitioners to assess the extent of parents' knowledge, confidence and skills in caring for children;
- outlines the things that are making family life hard to cope with and what might be put in place to make it better;
- looks at the impact on the child of how they are being cared for;
- gives or represents the child or young person's views about how life is for them.

The last two points will also be covered in the individual child's assessment but may also be included as part of the one that focuses on parenting.

The NSPCC factsheet 'Assessing Parenting Capacity' (2013) refers to the six parenting dimensions used in the *Framework for the Assessment of Children in Need and Their Families in England and Wales* (Department of Health, 2000). It suggests outlining parents' strengths and weaknesses in providing: basic care; ensuring safety; emotional warmth; stimulation; guidance and boundaries; and stability. The factsheet says that the impact of wider factors on parenting and the child's development should be included: for example, family history and functioning; extended family; housing; employment; income; social integration; and community resources (NSPCC, 2013). It advises that to get a full picture of parenting capacity, the practitioner should observe the care that parents provide in a variety of settings and at different times of the day (Jones, 2010) and also try to establish whether 'poor' parenting is a regular occurrence (Kellett and Apps, 2009).

There are clearly many ways in which this can be approached, and family support services and others who undertake parenting assessments either use accredited formats or devise their own, in order to cover the areas listed above.

Topic areas

The following topic areas were used by one third-sector service as a broad guide to undertaking parenting assessments, employing the visual tools described later in this chapter:

○ What does daily life look like?
○ Are there housing, financial and/or health problems that are having a bearing on parenting?
○ Are there other life skills which could be developed with support?
○ Are the parents' own childhoods and their knowledge of childcare influencing the care they are giving their children?
○ What are the relationships with child, parents (including resident and non-resident fathers), wider family and other supports?
○ Are children being supported to make the most of education? Have parents missed out on education themselves and why was this?

As part of these, service staff also considered:

○ Parents' openness (and ability) to be supported and to make changes.
○ Whether putting supports in place would be likely to enable the parent(s) to nurture and care for their child.

While planning and doing an assessment in a methodical way is desirable, practitioners know that plans often get disrupted by events and crises, and that they need to be flexible and creative. Situations occur which can tell practitioners a great deal about how the family 'works together' (or not) when facing problems and which offer opportunities to explore topics in a way which is not too prescriptive. The way in which the assessment is done, and the tools that can be used to do it, can be important in ensuring parents feel they are active participants.

Using visual tools for assessment

> 'Looking at the clock of what our day was like yesterday really brought home to me how much time I was sleeping during the day – what was my son doing then? I realized then how much our night-time routines needed to change.' Parent, study D

In our experience, parents may feel more able to take an active part in the assessment process if visual tools are used to help the discussion, rather than by referring to a lengthy checklist of questions. The use of visual tools to promote discussion means that responses are likely to be more detailed than they would be if only questions are asked. Each parent's responses will need to be written up in a more concise way in the assessment report.

The following six sessions were devised by practitioners in one family support service to cover the main topic areas required for the parenting assessment. These were primarily used as a guideline, as they sometimes led to other areas of discussion which needed to be covered, perhaps at a later stage. Flexibility was required in planning their order.

The assessment of the child takes place alongside this one and involves the child more directly, depending on their age.

Session 1: Our Day Yesterday

Aims

To look at daily routines and activities to get a picture of what daily life looks like for parents and children; may give helpful information about health (sleep, diet, activities), moods and stresses; how much the family does together and how they relax; what is NOT included; drug and alcohol use may come up with prompts.

Method

The parent attaches the activity flashcards, such as 'waking up' next to the time on the Velcro pads around the outside of the clock. The emotion flashcards allow us to see how the parent feels at certain points throughout the day – when is the most stressful or difficult time or when does the service user feel at their most relaxed? How do parents/children feel at these times? What do they enjoy together and what leads to arguments?

Resources

○ Two 'Our Day' clocks – one for morning and one for afternoon and evening (and possible later use of 'Ideal Day' clocks to look at how things could be)
○ Velcro-backed, post-it notes to surround the clock 'activity' and 'emotions' flashcards

Notes

Looking at a specific day (such as yesterday) usually offers more detail than a 'general' day.

Practitioners found that, by using the clock with parents again at a later stage, they could plan any support required to reduce stressful times and plan the day differently: for example, to include more time spent with children in shared activities. Parents often found that the visual methods helped them find their own solutions for reducing stress at particular times of day.

Session 2: Everyday life

Aims

To look at housing and housing needs; money management – income, budgeting, debts; other day-to-day life skills including cooking; employment and training.

Methods

House picture exercise: Ask the parents what ten words describe the feelings in their home. Can they see any scope for change in the future?

Pit and ladder exercise: Lay out the picture of the pit, with the bulldozer piling rubble into the pit. Ask the parent to think about things which get them down and write these on the pieces of rubble, which are falling into the pit. Ask the parent to draw a ladder leading out of the pit and together work out ways to get out of the pit, writing these on the ladder. Think about other times they felt at the bottom of the pit – what worked for getting out, then?

Outcomes Star: The points on the star can be agreed by parent and practitioner and can be used to measure how these aspects of their lives are now and what could be done to improve them, if necessary.

Resources
- Picture of a house for the House picture exercise
- Drawing of a pit with a bulldozer, one of a ladder and separate individual paper boulders for Pit and ladder exercise
- An Outcomes Star with space for practical areas as the points on the star

Notes

The Outcomes Star is licensed for use, and workers should be trained in introducing the materials (www.outcomesstar.org.uk/wp-content/uploads/Family-Star-Plus-User-Guide-Preview.pdf; accessed 6 January 2018)

Session 3: Getting to know you and your family

Aims

To discuss and explore family relationships and their feelings about themselves and family members. Who are the people in their family? How often do they see them? What sort of relationship is it? Is it a helpful one to them in bringing up their children, and in what ways? Or if not, why is this?

Methods

Parent cards: Use 'post-it' notes to add parents' words to describe themselves – what they like and what they dislike.

Family tree/eco-map: With themselves in the middle, use the person-shaped cards to place family members and descriptive and emotion flashcards (how they make the parent feel) for each person OR circle the pre-written descriptive and emotions words on the 'Getting to know your family' sheets.

Resources

○ Two cut-out shapes of parent
○ Family eco-map and/or family tree; laminated cards of women, men, children; flashcards with descriptive words and pictures
○ Emotions cards: Three A4 cards with silhouette cut-outs of people and pre-written and blank descriptive words cards OR 'Getting to know your family' sheets with descriptive and emotions words

Notes

This session can be done in parallel with both parents and child separately or as a family.

Session 4: Bringing up children

Aims

To discuss what the parent knows about how a child learns and develops. To explore their own childhood and what has influenced their ways of parenting? How did they learn to be a parent?

Methods

Quiz or developmental milestones ladder: Use to find out parents' expectations of children and their understanding of children's needs and abilities at each developmental stage, including their levels of understanding, play, learning and safety.

Life events snake or graph: Use to explore the effects of important events on the parent. A Life Events Timeline aimed at children can be found at www. thespruce.com/timeline-activity-for-kids-4145478 (accessed 6 January 2018).

Parenting checklist: Use the sixteen questions to help parents reflect on being a parent.

Parenting task snap cards: Use this game to explore the many tasks that parents do for their children and the skills these require.

House drawings: In one drawing, ask parents to write ten 'feelings' words about the home they grew up in; use the second drawing to describe what happens where in their current home (e.g. where people talk and eat); and the third one to think about what an 'ideal' home might look like.

Resources

- Quiz about what children can do at different ages and stages
- Developmental milestones ladder and statements about what children can do at different ages and stages
- Life events snake drawing/graph
- Parenting checklist
- Parenting task cards – snap game
- Three outline drawings of a house

Notes

The parenting checklist questions can be represented by pictures to make the exercise more interesting.

Session 5: My child

Aims

To find out more about their child, their relationship with them and how they communicate with and react to them, especially when they are upset. This session also includes discussions about the parent's attitudes to school and health.

Methods

'Picture of my child' exercise: Parents draw, write about and/or use photos to describe their child.

'My child' checklist: Has questions about what makes the child happy and upset and can be used together with the 'How I see my child' exercises.

'How I see my child' exercise (a): Uses pre-completed and blank flashcards with descriptive words to enable the parent to describe the child and the emotions they feel about them.

'How I see my child' exercise (b): Uses plastic balls with descriptive words about the child's behaviour and reactions and three containers labelled 'behaviour I feel good about', 'behaviour I find difficult' and 'behaviour I can cope with' into which the parent places the balls, to promote discussion and assist assessment of the parent's reaction to this.

School quiz: Use this illustrated quiz to explore what school was like for the parent (what they were good at, what they liked and did not like about it; how schools used to be) and also how schools have changed; what the child's experience is; and what the benefits of education can be.

Health quiz: This works in a similar way with topics on diet, exercise, physical and mental health. They quizzes both aim to promote discussion to assist assessment.

Resources

- ○ Drawing and writing materials for 'Picture of my child' exercise
- ○ 'My child' checklist
- ○ Containers, balls and flashcards for 'How I see my child' exercises
- ○ School: picture-based quiz
- ○ Health: picture-based quiz

Notes

The photos of the child, taken by parents, can help to illustrate the 'My child' checklist.

Session 6: Our family's wider world

Aims

To find out who is in the family's wider support network – family, friends and neighbours, as well as professionals and people from other organisations who provide support.

Methods

Network tree: Can be drawn by the parent and worker together to plot and discuss who the family look to for help.

Blob Tree: Enables parents to identify which branch they are sitting on (in relation to their supports) and to discuss the people and agencies who are around them. Parents can reflect on past and present support networks and how they do, or have, supported them and their children on a practical and personal level.

Resources

- ○ Personal network tree (or Blob Tree, below)
- ○ The Blob Tree and all its variations can be downloaded at www.blobtree. com (accessed 6 January 2018)

Notes

In common with all parts of the assessment process, painful emotions can be felt by parents: for example, when discussing the loss of loved ones. This should be taken into account when planning the length of sessions.

The 'Assessing and Promoting Resilience in Children' practice guides written by Brigid Daniel and Sally Wassell (Daniel and Wassell, 2002a; 2002b; 2002c) offer helpful and creative tools for use with parents and children, when assessing how parents are caring for and communicating with children, the impact on children of how they are being parented and the extent to which their resilience promoted by those around them.

In undertaking assessment work practitioners must make use of good observation skills and levels of 'emotional intelligence', being able to 'see' what is happening and 'tune into' situations, in particular to any risks which may be present for the child.

Analysis and support planning

Once the material for inclusion in the assessment report has been gathered, it should be written up in a way that enables descriptive information to form the basis of an analysis of the extent to which the child is safe and well in their day-to-day life. The wording of the report requires skill and sensitivity and must reflects parents' strengths and weaknesses while also being honest about any risks to the child.

From this, a plan can be formed of what could be put in place to enable parents to ensure their child's safety and welfare. We know that careful analysis based on well-formed judgements are crucially important, and there are a number of books that aim to help practitioners to achieve this difficult task (e.g. Milner and O'Byrne, 2002; Helm, 2011.

Our purpose in this book is to note what parents told us was important to them about the content of the assessment report – both the detail of the information gathered and the way in which it is used to analyse what supports are needed to help them to care for their child. Their main concern was that it should be written clearly and in language that they understood, and also that it honestly reflected what they had said during the assessment.

Not all parents will agree with the final outcome of the assessment. If practitioners are clear and give solid examples of why they have come to a decision, it will help parents to understand and accept the subsequent outcome, even if this results in their child being removed from their care. Parents' voices should, nonetheless, be heard, even when this is difficult to manage because professionals are having to make a judgement call about risk and risk management.

Any proposed support plan must also make sense and be acceptable to families if it has a good chance of succeeding; it also needs to include a sufficient level of support, particularly in the early stages:

'I was offered help for twelve weeks but I needed more time and they were able to offer me more. It needs to be at the right pace for parents.' Parent, study H

Having said that, there do need to be signs of change within timescales that are acceptable to ensure the child's well-being. Extended support is usually offered if there are such indications signs.

It is also important for practitioners to remember that the process of assessment is dynamic and ongoing. The family's situation will change, and many factors will influence how children are cared for. Practitioners reassess how life is for both children and parents every time they have contact with them and should be sensitive to, and ask about, any changes. For example, parents told us that there will usually be reasons for visible signs of deterioration in their home, or for them struggling to cope with care of their children, so it is important for practitioners to ask about this:

'Rather than say your house is slipping again (into a mess) why can't they say 'what's going on with you?'' Parent, study G

The contact we have with the family while offering support gives us many opportunities to continually reassess the risks and protective factors for children. These should always be noted to inform ongoing reviews of the assessment.

In the next chapter we write about a possible way of approaching and structuring family support, while also taking into account the family's individual needs. The structure we suggest was devised by practitioners, based partly on parents' feedback about what they felt they needed in relation to family support.

Summary points

❏ The assessment is crucial in ensuring that the child is safe and well and in deciding what types of support can be put in place to help parents care for their child. Some parents felt that the assessment became an end in itself and did not always lead to the proposed support plan being put in place in an effective way.

❏ Fathers, stepfathers and other primary carers, including those not living with the child, should be included in the assessment, even if doing so is not straightforward and requires careful planning. Many fathers say they feel left out of the assessment and planning processes for their children.

❏ Parents told us that the language used when undertaking and writing up the assessment must make sense to them, so that they feel fully involved in it. If parents play an active part in designing the support plan, and it is realistic, it will have more chance of success.

❏ There are a range of helpful assessment frameworks which practitioners use, and the visual materials can help the assessment 'come alive' for some parents.

❏ Parents appreciated practitioners being alert to changes in their situation and emotional well-being, and asking them about this if it showed up in indirect ways.

CHAPTER 4

What do parents say they need?

'When you first get the baby you think – what do I do with this? You are clueless. Sometimes you can ask a health visitor but they disappear too quickly.' Parent, study G

Introduction

This chapter outlines what parents told us about receiving support from professionals, and what helped them most when they were finding it hard to care for their children. We recognise that parents are not the only 'experts' in this; practitioners use their professional training and judgement when assessing families' needs and planning support for them. Children's and young people's views about what they need are also important and were represented in many of our research studies, alongside those of parents. Our purpose here is to reflect what parents said to us, while accepting that this is not the whole picture. We know that effective 'engagement' with parents is crucial if family support is to succeed (Davies and Ward, 1995), and their views and preferences are clearly valid (Quinton, 2004).

What parents highlighted was their need for knowledge and information, provided in a way that made sense to them, and for opportunities to build their confidence and their skills in caring for their children. We have, therefore, chosen to structure this chapter around these three main themes. In some ways, these three themes can be seen as a process – once parents know more about what their children need, help can be given to build parents' confidence, so that this learning can be put into practice and support then offered to develop the skills required. However, in practice, these aspects of support take place alongside one another.

The influence of environment

In our work with families, we have found that some parents find it hard to prioritise the care of their children if their physical environment is inadequate, and this is even more the case if this is affecting their mental health. Parents told us that they can become depressed and distracted if their family is living in insecure and unsuitable housing, if they are worried about not having enough money to feed, clothe and keep their children warm and if it feels as though there is no prospect of their situation improving. Parents said that, when they are under pressure, they can at times lose sight of some of the important things that children need. Some may find it hard to provide the basics such as food, heating and clothing – if parents are preoccupied with worries about coping with everyday life, other needs children have for emotional warmth, encouragement and stimulation may require more effort and energy than they can find.

And, as one practitioner put it, 'there's no point in discussing bedtime routines if the child has no bed'.

> 'Practical help with housing is so important – if your flat is damp, you can end up spending all your money on heating.'
> Parent, study C

Practitioners can support parents to access help from agencies such as housing and welfare benefits. This may have to be prioritised before 'parenting' work can take place. By going along with parents to other services and supporting them to ask for what they require need, they can be helped to find the confidence to do this on their own, once formal supports have come to an end.

The spectrum of support needs

The parents whose views we have included in this book had become involved with support services for a range of reasons, and their circumstances varied greatly. Some had children who had been taken into care and had poor opinions of social work practitioners; others were on the edge of having their children removed from their care. Some parents were finding it hard to cope because of temporary difficulties which, with some extra help, could probably be addressed. Other parents were misusing drugs and alcohol. Some were finding their involvement with statutory services difficult and needed help from mediating agencies to help them to cope with this:

'The support staff know me well – they know it takes me time to mull things over. They know how to calm me down and they listen to me when I rant on. I think my head would explode without them.' Parent, study C

However, families' circumstances and needs do change, and practitioners must be constantly attuned to these changes. Even if parents seem on the surface to be co-operating and doing what is asked of them, there may be pressures and problems bubbling away just out of sight. Every contact practitioners have with a family is an opportunity to assess the risks for children, and they must be alert to any warning signs that appear.

When chronologies are examined as part of Serious Case Reviews, we see how often opportunities are missed to ensure a child's safety (Vincent, 2010; Brandon *et al.*, 2012). Practitioners who are providing support need to ensure that they see the children regularly, notice if there are strangers in the house, pick up on parents' moods and children's behaviour and note if there has been a deterioration in the condition of the home, exploring with parents why this might be. Families' needs may initially seem relatively straightforward but may turn out to be more complex as practitioners get to know them better. Whatever the circumstances, practitioners must be alert to changes and use the support-based relationship they have formed to ask difficult and challenging questions of parents, if this becomes necessary.

What parents say is important: The practitioner's manner and approach

'We sometimes feel patronised and made to feel small by professionals – sometimes you make us feel that we can't ever be a good parent. We need encouragement so we don't end up feeling that we'll never move forward. The best social workers understand why we are stressed, are straight with us and encourage us when we do well. When they go out of our lives we really miss them.' Parent consultant, study F

Parents told us how demeaning it can be to feel judged or made to feel inferior or inadequate. We mentioned earlier the importance that parents placed on professionals listening to them, understanding them and being honest with them. Building a relationship is a crucial aspect of providing support and an important social work skill (Munro, 2011). However, this takes time, and it is worth spending as much time as possible in the early stages of offering support to try to do this. This may be difficult for professionals with a high workload, but it should pay dividends over time. It could make a difference as to whether parents are actively and meaningfully involved in the support provided, not only seeing scope for change but also feeling able to accept any 'challenging' conversations that practitioners think are needed (e.g. about the level of childcare parents are providing). Being clear about the boundaries of the relationship – ensuring it is warm but professional – is something parents said they appreciated, too.

Providing the level and types of support we outline in this chapter may feel daunting for practitioners who are working with a large number of families. If time is short, we suggest that they identify the priorities for the family and try to use some of our suggestions within what is realistic for their role. We recognise that this is not easy. But parents tell us that what we describe here can be effective in helping them so the time required may be well spent.

Practitioners clearly may not be able to provide every type of support a family needs on their own. It is usually possible to draw on the support of staff from other services, even if this is only to seek advice and relay it to the family. Practitioners need to balance making use of other support services, and introducing too many professionals to a family, with the risk of them becoming overwhelmed, as we touched on earlier:

> 'I didn't think family support would be any use to me – I've got too many workers. It's confusing and it takes up too much time. But then I changed my mind and thought it was worth giving it a go for my son's sake.' Parent, study J

Working with fathers

Some of the parents and carers whose views are represented in this book were fathers, stepfathers, grandfathers and uncles, providing care for children on their own or with partners. Some of these male carers were receiving support from family support services that were designed specifically for men and typically included male support staff. We know that men often feel more comfortable talking with male practitioners than female ones (Ghate *et al.*, 2000). Other men were being supported by services aimed at parents in general, and were taking part either with partners or alone. Fathers and other male carers who are involved with these non-gendered services are usually greatly outnumbered by women – both practitioners and other parents. It requires sensitivity and consideration of men's needs to support them in ways that keep them involved and are relevant to their experiences of the parenthood.

Some of what fathers told us about their experiences of support services was similar to what mothers said. One group we talked with greatly appreciated the fathers' group they attended but those receiving support from general parenting support services also valued the help they received and did not say if they thought that men-only support would have made their experiences different. There are a number of practice-based reports and books available which provide useful advice about ways of supporting men with their parenting role (Clapton, 2013; FaHCSIA, 2009).

Knowledge: What parents say they need to know

> 'It's important to realize that some of us haven't had very good childhoods ourselves. We don't know what children need from their parents – we don't know how to look after them very well or how to play with them. So we need clear information and advice, using language that makes sense to us.' Parent consultant, study F

A number of parents told us about their lack of opportunity to learn from others about looking after children. Some knowledge and awareness are needed to develop parenting skills, and practitioners cannot make assumptions about how much parents know about the multiple things involved in caring for children. In their training, practitioners learn about childcare and development – however, as those of us who have children know, the reality of looking after them is very different. Much of what parents bring to raising their children will depend on what sort of childhood they themselves had and what those who looked after them or other adults in their lives provided by way of a nurturing role model.

Some parents talked about what they saw as the lack of 'a manual' about caring for children, and how they thought this would be useful. They did, however, recognise that all children are individuals and react differently to situations. In fact, we know in the past many parents did make use of childcare books, such as those written by Dr Spock and Dr Miriam Stoppard. Many now look on mumsnet and similar sites on the Internet – however, this is not the natural place for all parents to turn. Others ask their friends and family, but we know that many parents are isolated and have no one they can talk to about their childcare worries. Some would not approach even close friends and family, because they fear being seen as inadequate – they think that parenting is just something they should know how to do. Many will do as their own parents did and not question whether this made them feel happy and secure during their own childhoods and enable them to become well-rounded adults.

Reflective exercise

Have you ever thought about how you were parented or where you learnt to be a parent, if you have children? Do you think your parent, or whoever cared for you, did a good job? If you are a parent or carer, who were your role models? Have you chosen to parent or care for a child differently from your own parents or carers?

Imparting knowledge

The adversities that many parents have experienced have left many of them lacking confidence and, if coupled with gaps in schooling, may also mean that their levels of literacy and numeracy are not high. This can have a major impact on some aspects of their childcare, including such basic but important things as following written directions about giving medicines and making meals. In helping parents to learn more about what children need from them, practitioners must make sure that they adapt the ways they do this to the learning style best suited to individual parents.

Reinforcing and reassuring

Parents told us that they often need to be shown or told, more than once, how to undertake some aspects of childcare. For new parents, this may include how to hold their baby safely, make up a bottle, wash and change their baby's nappy and how to soothe their baby if he or she cries a lot. If their baby is displaying withdrawal symptoms from maternal drug use during pregnancy, they may need repeated practical support with administering medication. Parents said that they need reassurance that it is okay to be shown an important task such as this, a number of times; some said that it helped to know that many other parents need this, too. They told us they appreciate staff being patient and taking time to explain things in a way that is not patronising or judgemental:

> 'The support staff don't make me feel shy or insecure. I can talk to them about everything – not just about my son but about relationships and things. They treat me with respect and give my son lots of attention.' Parent, study J

Parents also said they appreciated practical help as well as emotional support – again, coupled with reassurance that many other parents also need this. Practical and emotional help is discussed in more detail later in this chapter in the section on developing parents' skills.

Family support practitioners also have a role in re-affirming health visitor advice. Parents told us that it was not helpful to have different support workers suggesting contradictory ways of doing things. Health visitors provide written guidance about many aspects of childcare, such as weaning, safe sleeping and nappy changing, and if practitioners are up to date with current health advice there is less chance of contradictory information being given. It also helps, parents told us, if family support workers develop a good rapport with other professionals working in childcare and make good use of other services whose staff might be able to help:

> 'The staff seem to work closely with my health visitor, nursery and school. I've not got a good relationship with the school and she's helping with this. So she's a sort of bridge – but more than a bridge – she is part of the structure too.' Parent, study H

Parents said that they have more confidence in support workers who are well-informed about the age and stage of development of their child. If support workers are uncertain about anything parents ask them, they would prefer workers to ask other professionals rather than feel they have to know everything and respond immediately to every query.

Learning about what children need

The place of parenting programmes

> 'I was cynical about coming to a group-based dad's course but not only have I learnt lots of practical information and skills, which improve my confidence as a father, I really enjoyed discussing the role of a father. The group discussion was very open and let us ask questions and explore topics. I'd come back for more.' Parent, study P

There are numerous structured parenting programmes in use across the UK, many of which have been described and evaluated in other books (Moran *et al.*, 2004; Lindsay and Cullen, 2011; Donkin, 2014). They include the Positive Parenting Programme (known as Triple P), Mellow Parenting and The Incredible Years, although there are many others. Some parents told us that they had enjoyed these and that at least parts of the content had been helpful. Some liked the experience of getting together with other parents to share stories and learn about strategies for coping with children's behaviour. They found that it helped to know that they were not the only parents who were struggling with the demands of caring for children.

However, other parents said they found taking part in a group-based structured programme difficult; some had problems getting out to programmes at set times, and others felt nervous about meeting other people and preferred one-to-one sessions with a practitioner. Talking about this more personal approach, one parent said:

> 'It's been very different than I thought. I like the individual aspect and that it's not in a group. It's more about me and building my confidence than all about being a parent.' Parent, study J

Making learning enjoyable and useful

Structured parenting programmes are often followed or adapted for use with individual families, tailored to their particular situation. However, some parents found it hard to cope with structured programmes, even if these took place on a one-to-one basis. They spoke highly of other activities that support staff did with them, which made learning about caring for children more enjoyable and meaningful for them. Practitioners had used imaginative ways to encourage parents to think about what their children needed, using 'hands-on' approaches that made them feel fully involved in their learning. These activities were designed to be fun and informal and helpful to parents whose learning styles were not well-adapted to written or even verbal methods.

Where possible, many of these were undertaken together with the children. These would happen initially with staff, usually but not always in the family home or a playroom in a family centre. As their confidence increased, parents were encouraged to try some of the activities out at home.

Including partners was also important:

> 'I liked that the support includes the whole family – my partner and my older child. My partner is all for it – he was there when we discussed what sort of help we could get and he was the one who said "let's go for it".' Parent, study J

Example 1: Knowledge about child development

Practitioners must do what they can to keep parents interested and involved when discussing children's developmental needs at various stages of their lives by being creative and making the process of learning enjoyable. There are many interactive materials available to help with this, or else practitioners can design their own, using pictures from magazines to draw colourful charts which illustrate what children can be expected to do and how we can respond to them.

Parents who were misusing drugs and alcohol told us that they were sometimes not aware of how their drug and alcohol use could have an impact on their child's development and feelings of safety. As well as talking about the negative impacts of substance use, it can also be effective to help parents think about how they can manage their substance use in order for them to keep their child safe and healthy. By taking this approach, parents said they were sometimes more open to accepting the supports being offered:

> 'I hardly seen my wee boy, I used to give him money to go out and play so that I could take my stuff. I didn't play games or anything with him. He didn't always get to school, sometimes I would get up and take him but he more often wasn't there; his

attendance at that time was 58%. I was too high all the time to keep my house clean; it was chaos. My partner sold drugs so I used to go and drop them off and collect the money or I would sit at home smoking crack along with other people. People came in and out of my house – it was mad. I did some life-story work with the family worker and that re-enforced for me how bad things where and that's what hit the nail on the head. That, and the fact that my son had to repeat Primary 1. It was my big wakeup call – I thought 'what have I done to my son'? Parent, study D

Family example: Carol

Carol had experienced neglect as a child and used drugs and alcohol to try to cope with her depression and anxiety. Her son Alan, aged six, was showing destructive behaviour in and out of school. As support workers got to know the family, they realised that Alan watched a lot of adult content in TV and films, and that this was having an impact on his language and behaviour. Support was offered to help Carol understand the affect this was having on him and his need to feel parented rather than see his mum as a 'friend'. She was supported to set reasonable boundaries and given encouragement to stick with these, although this was very difficult at first. Using the SHANARRI (safe, healthy, achieving, nurtured, active, respected, responsible and include) well-being indicators as a guide (Scottish Government, 2008), Carol was supported to understand Alan's needs and develop ways to meet them.

Example 2: Knowledge about health and well-being
Parents told us that they enjoyed learning and thinking about different ways to improve their own and their children's health; this included their emotional health and well-being, as well as their physical health. What they found most helpful and enjoyable were informal and fun opportunities to do this. They liked taking part in discussions about what sort of food and activities their family would most enjoy. Again, the use of quizzes and pictures can help to stimulate these discussions about the options, taking into account the family's circumstances and family members' interests, likes and dislikes.

If possible to arrange, practical sessions that focus on healthy cooking and preparation of healthy meals and snacks can be enjoyed by parents and children together. If practitioners have access to a kitchen, in a family centre or similar, buying food and making meals together and then eating them with the family can be a good way of building relationships. It can also be a good opportunity to improve literacy and numeracy skills, by reading through instructions and weighing out ingredients.

Some parents told us that they had become anxious about their homes being clean and in tip-top order for visiting professionals. They felt that it would help them if professionals needed were clearer that a stimulating environment for a child is more important than one that is hoovered and tidied every morning. Parents said they required tips about how to provide an interesting and safe environment for their child. They may need reassurance that this is not just about orderliness but also about a living space in which children feel comfortable and relaxed and able to play:

> 'Sometimes social workers give us confusing messages like saying our houses should be clean and tidy but then we're wrong because we haven't got toys on the floor.' Parent consultant, study F

Giving parents and children the opportunity to get involved in activities that promote their well-beiluded sport activities and leisurely walks in parks, talking and noticing whng was also important to parents. They enjoyed family outings that incat was going on around them. These conversations helped to counterbalance some of the negative exchanges which take place in some families who are under stress. It is helpful to research activities with parents and find ones that do not cost the family prohibitive amounts of money.

Example 3: Emotional literacy (including family communication and bonding)

Some parents said that the support work made them realise that they were not good at reading their children's feelings; for some, this was due to their own childhood experiences of lack of consideration being shown about their feelings:

> 'I learnt how to talk to my daughter and listen to her and find out what matters to her. I realized I didn't know her very well at all.' Parent, study B

Emotional literacy work includes activities to help family members to see things from the point of view of others in the family, appreciate their feelings, find ways to talk things over and express feelings and emotions. Parents learn why children respond in certain ways to the manner in which they talk to them. Building the skills to react differently is the next step (see p. 67):

> 'I can understand better now why children act in certain ways, like trashing their rooms when their mum gets sentenced (to prison). We learnt tips about talking to our children, even on the phone – like asking them open questions and getting the conversation going.' Parent, study B

Family example: Rose

Rose was a mother of two children under fifteen. She was serving a short sentence in prison for drug-related offences, and her children were living with relatives. In between previous periods in custody, they had at times been in homeless accommodation. Rose took part in emotional literacy work during her sentence, as part of which she was shown a hard-hitting video made by children. She commented: 'The videos brought home how it felt for the children – like mine, always on the move from house to house and losing all our things. It opened my eyes, how it was for them and never giving them time to say what it was like from their point of view. It was upsetting to see the video but I had to face it.'

Building confidence in parenting

> 'I can sometimes be under-confident and my support worker has helped build my confidence without me realising it. She points out the good in you and the positives – she encourages me, saying "you are doing well with your kids" – that helps.' Parent, study H

In our discussions with parents, a common theme was how many of them experienced low levels of self-esteem and confidence. The majority of parents we worked with, or met in the course of undertaking research, told us how they lacked confidence in many aspects of their daily lives:

> 'When I went out I was always anxious on buses and at the shops – I couldn't go into crowds at all. So the support worker

came with me and showed me it could be okay and now I can go into town and even be in a crowd.' Parent, study H

There are many reasons why parents experienced low self-esteem and lack of belief in themselves. Some talked about their childhoods and feeling overly criticised and not being praised or encouraged. Childhood neglect or living in a violent or unhappy household had resulted in anxiety and depression. In some cases, parents (usually, but not always, women) were subject to violence in their adult lives or were in a relationship that led to conflict and resulted in their confidence levels being low.

Whatever the reasons, having little confidence in their abilities as a parent had numerous spin-offs. Feelings of self-doubt meant they felt unable to carry things through: for example, in setting behaviour boundaries for their children:

> 'I learnt that kids pick up on big and tiny things that are going on in their mum's life and that it affects their behaviour and can put everything up in the air. Our relationship is more positive as I am more confident. Before, I was worried that I was being bad to him if I said "no".' Parent, study A

Many parents expressed anxiety about talking with other people, particularly people they had not met before, and some found it hard to venture outside their local area or even leave their home:

> 'I tend to hide in my house – I don't go out and socialize because people can be cruel and nasty. My support worker has boosted my confidence – it's hard to explain – it's what she says and does. She says things which make me feel good about myself and showed me that people can be alright. I pick up my child from nursery now and have made a good friend from that.' Parent, study J

Not surprisingly, this lack of confidence extended to how many of them felt about their parenting abilities. They talked about being unsure about how to care for children as they got older and their needs changed, and, even if they knew, worried that they were not getting it right:

> 'The help I have received from the support staff has been vital for my children and myself. I'm a lot more positive and I have

a lot more coping strategies and parenting skills. I am sorting my addiction problems and I'm even more confident about new situations. I am changing areas in my life that I would not have even attempted to change six months ago.' Parent, study D

Much anxiety was expressed about what other people thought of what they saw as their inadequate parenting skills and of being 'shown up' in public if their children misbehaved:

'She helped me break through the barrier. I react to my children better and I learnt not to be over-anxious and that it doesn't matter what other people think of you. It has had a ripple effect.' Parent, study H

Some parents explained how they knew they came across to professionals as defensive or aggressive, but that this was partly due to lack of confidence. This can be hard for practitioners to disentangle, and it takes confidence on their part to try to get below the surface of what can often feel like a threatening situation. Hostility can also be masking very real feelings of fear – fear not only of being judged, but also of the implications of social work involvement and the powers social workers have to remove children from their homes.

Family example: Mary

Mary was the mother of Joe, aged eight. Joe's father had died a year before from a drug overdose, following which Mary had suffered severe depression and her confidence had been severely shaken. She was sure everyone was talking about her, and she had little support. Mary was finding it hard to care for Joe and give him the attention he needed. Joe was seeking attention through his behaviour. Family support included help for Joe to talk about his loss through specialised play sessions. Mary was given encouragement to express her emotions and recognise what Joe needed from her as a parent. Parent and child play sessions then helped them to reforge the bond between them. Mary's confidence increased as Joe started to respond to her and, with help, she started to attend a playgroup where she got to know another mother who supported her.

Fostering parenting skills: building on knowledge and confidence

> 'It helps if they show us how to be better parents, not just tell us where we are going wrong.' Parent, study F

Once parents have a better understanding of their children's needs and have started to gain more confidence in their ability to provide care for their children, they told us that they felt more able, with support, to start putting into practice some of the skills required to care for them in a more nurturing way:

> 'To start with I thought support would just be them coming out every week or two and talking about things but it's not been like that. They come out when you need them and spend time with you and your children – actually doing things with you.' Parent, study H

Parents told us that they found it helpful if practitioners demonstrated skills by role modelling: for example, how best to react to children when they were being unco-operative. They could then try these skills out with the practitioner present and then later on their own. Parents said they appreciated being given really practical strategies and having things spelt out. It was helpful if practitioners said: 'Try saying ... in x situation'. 'Try doing y when child displays z behaviour'. 'Try it again, and again, this has worked for many other families in a similar situation.'

It was important that techniques for staying calm were used when parents felt under pressure, with their children present. This was not always possible, and other tools might need to be used:

> 'The videos were good which showed you the right and wrong ways of dealing with situations, such as kids wanting things in the supermarket. You need to try a certain tone of voice and try to compromise.' Parent, study A

Example 1: Communication and understanding feelings
Parents talked about sessions that used games, drawings, miming, role play and storytelling to help them think about the effect of how they talked to children and also to other adults in the family:

'My support worker has shown me how to communicate with the children in a less emotional way. They are really not bad at all – it's more me because of my anxiety and depression. If my daughter had temper tantrums I couldn't cope with them – but I can now.' Parent, study H

Some parents admitted that they were not always able to think before they spoke, particularly in the heat of the moment, but were trying hard to talk things over with their children and not let emotions get the upper hand:

'I don't shout as much now. I stop and explain to the boys why they can't do things. They don't always respond but more often than not they do. I can see when it's escalating and try to stop it.' Parent, study H

It was important to parents that support workers offered ongoing reassurance that improvements were taking place:

'I admit I do let the parenting skills slip – I seem to lose focus but the staff always encourage me and tell me how well I've been doing. It helps me feel positive and helps me get things moving along.' Parent, study D

Most parents felt that they had seen good results from the strategies they tried:

'What do I do at home now? Well, the praise thing – that works with him. Also asking him what he would like to do – he loves that. And the reward chart, that's a good thing. Sometimes you realise you are shouting at them but shouting doesn't work. You need to give them a quiet warning instead. There's also planned ignoring – that can be hard. You learn a lot from this parenting work.' Parent, study D

Example 2: Learning to play

Some parents explained that, as children, they had little or no experience of playing with adults. They said they needed to be shown how to play, and some felt embarrassed and lacking in confidence to let their guard down and act in what they saw as a child-like way. They enjoyed opportunities to experience what fun play can be and realise the important part it has in helping them to form a bond with their children.

Some parents had not been read to as children and were new to the idea of reading as a shared and nurturing experience. It was particularly hard for those who lacked reading skills and, for some, it was an incentive to start adult literacy classes.

For some parents, lack of finances was seen as a barrier to play and activity time with their children. Encouraging parents to spend time with their children in ways that do not involve spending money is important. So while it can be useful for practitioners to be equipped with books and toys when visiting families for play sessions, practitioners can also demonstrate play in the family home using items that are readily available, such as wooden spoons, pots and pans – things that form the basis for what is known as 'heuristic play'. Parents can offer their children the opportunity to explore real-life, everyday objects, helping them to discover the world around them. This is particularly useful for young babies; for older children, the opportunity to colour in or do art and craft activities together with their parents can be fun. Be warned – playing board games may need some careful management at first, depending on the competitive streak of parents who find they enjoy the feeling of winning:

> 'Our support worker comes up with ideas about play and activities with the children and ideas like a glow jar which my daughter painted and takes to bed with her and it has helped her get to sleep.' Parent, study J

Offering parents the chance to participate in adult-focused art and craft groups can be particularly helpful in increasing their confidence and in using such sessions to speak freely about their own inhibitions in relation to the important aspect of promoting play at home. Practitioners have a role in re-enforcing the message that play and time spent having fun together are both possible and important. Parents were often unclear about what was available to them in their local community, and anxious about going along. Practitioners may need to accompany parents to parent-and-toddler groups or stay-and-play sessions, with a view to gradually reducing their involvement as parents get to know other people.

Family example: Tony

Tony was not sure about how to play with Sammy, his two-year-old daughter, and lacked the confidence to try. Tony had been neglected as a child and did not remember his parents playing or spending much time with him. Social workers were involved with the family, and Tony was fearful of Sammy being removed from his care. Sammy was always dressed in an immaculate way. Tony was reluctant to allow Sammy to take part in finger painting and other messy activities at the nursery, even with a child apron on. He was not comfortable about getting messy or helping Sammy to paint. He was fearful of being judged as neglecting Sammy or having a dirty child.

Tony needed lots of encouragement and reassurance to accept that it was okay to get messy and to put Sammy in clothes that could be easily washed. After discussions about the benefits of play and spending time doing this with his daughter, Tony became more confident in playing with her and started to enjoy play sessions and having fun activities together.

Example 3: Routines and boundaries

Parents talked about the parts of the day when caring for children could be stressful, but many found it hard to put in place routines that would help with this. Early morning, especially with school-aged children, and bedtimes were the most difficult. It was a big help to parents if support workers not only discussed with them what might work for their family but also came out and demonstrated how to put this into action:

> 'Our support worker came out to help with the children's bed-times and get a routine in place – it took hours to start with. We now follow it ourselves without her but she sometimes texts in the evenings to check that things are okay.' Parent, study H

While it is not usually feasible for practitioners to offer intensive support to families on a long-term basis, the amount and type of support offered can be gradually phased out. The use of texting and some forms of social media can play a role, if they are used with caution. While not a substitute for face-to-face contact, they have their place, if ground rules for their use can be agreed between parent and practitioner:

> 'Staff helped me to get organised in the mornings, just after I had my baby I was on my own and I felt stressed I wasn't managing; I felt like throwing in the towel. The staff would help me in the morning to get both kids organised – they didn't do the work for me but they watched me and worked alongside me, then they would make sure I got Nicholas up to school. This gradually moved from every day to every other day till

eventually the support moved to telephone calls. I thought at that point I must be doing something right.' Parent, study D

When boundaries have not been set for children early on, it is harder for parents to enforce them as children have learnt how to engineer a situation whereby they can do as they please – and who can blame them? Support workers can demonstrate by their words and actions what is and what is not acceptable behaviour and language from children. They can also try to impress on parents the importance of sticking to 'the rules' in a consistent way:

> 'My support worker showed me how to cope with my daughter's behaviour, and major things have changed. She showed me how to avoid getting into big arguments with her and getting her to have a quiet time if she was kicking off. Not the naughty step as she used to go wild but quiet drawing on a special chair. She is in her own bed and I don't have to lie down with her until she goes to sleep.' Parent, study H

Family example: Robert and Pam

Robert and Pam were finding it hard to manage their three-year-old daughter's, Kirsty, angry and destructive behaviour. They lacked confidence in putting boundaries and strategies in place to prevent her outbursts, and the atmosphere in the home was tense and full of conflict. They avoided leaving the house with her, as they did not feel able to manage her outbursts. The support they received centred around role-modelling routines and techniques for responding to her. As the situation improved, it became possible to talk with Robert and Pam about the reasons for Kirsty's distressed behaviour, and they were able to start working on aspects of their own relationship which had been causing conflict. The home started to become a more calm and nurturing environment for all.

Example 4: Budgeting, shopping and cooking for a family
Parents said how hard it was on a limited income to stay within a budget for bills, including food and other necessities. It could be hard to accept advice and help to manage the household budget differently, and it often took some time before parents felt enough trust in their support worker to allow them to help with this. Once they did, they looked together

at meal plans for the week, at ways to save money by shopping differently: for example, by going to larger shops; and by trying out recipes that involved cheaper and, if possible, more healthy ingredients. Children were encouraged to try different food in schools, and this could be extended to meals at home, too.

Example 5: Encouraging learning

Most parents said they wanted their children to have greater opportunities than they felt they had themselves in their earlier lives. School had not been a good experience for many of them, and they had not been able to see the value of education. Some took the view that their children would follow the same path as them, and there was little point to having hope or ambition that things could be different. Others felt things could be different for both themselves and their children:

> 'I know that I could have done better as a parent but what I need is for you to offer me hope.' Parent consultant, study F

Some family support services have a role in encouraging parents' involvement in schoolwork by arranging joint parent-and-child homework sessions and by supporting regular contact between home and school. Some parents told us that, once they see how much their children enjoy learning, they start to recognise the benefits themselves and can be inspired to enrol in a college course, think about a part-time job or do some training, perhaps starting to fulfil ambitions they may have had at an earlier stage of their lives. If this can be sustained, this can boost the confidence and social networks of parents and, in turn, the whole family.

There are programmes of 'family learning' in some areas, which provide tutors and materials to encourage parents and children to learn together. There are other schemes, such as Vox Liminis (www.voxliminis.co.uk; accessed 6 January 2018), which aim to bring families closer together through the use of games and stories, poetry and art.

Nurseries sometimes provide extra support for children through nurture rooms and corners, and this may also include opportunities for parenting work on an individual or group basis:

> 'I've been given good advice about my daughter's behaviour – she can be hyper and fidget – and how to handle it. The nurture staff always try to help – they're really supportive here.' Parent, study M

Parallel work with children

Most of the examples described above involved parents undertaking activities aimed at trying out different ways of caring for children, and often doing this together with their children. Some children also took part in separate activities, which were designed to run alongside the support being offered to their parents. Some of these took place in schools and were run by school staff or by family support workers who came into school. Others involved social worker staff and therapists. Parents talked to us about the value of much of this work for their children; however, as our main purpose in this book is to reflect the views of parents about the support they themselves received, we do not include these activities here.

Providing family support

Parents and practitioners told us that receiving and providing support, if pitched in the right way and approached with a spirit of co-operation, can be both effective and enjoyable. It can include periods when progress feels slow and that it is not achieving change quickly enough, or to the extent required. There do have to be signs of improvement within time-scales that ensure children are not at risk of being unsafe or neglected. It can be hard for practitioners to end support to parents with whom good relationships have been built but who are unable, for whatever reason, to manage sufficient change. The need to remove children from their care will be emotional for all involved and, in these circumstances, support is required for children, parents and practitioners alike.

However, there are many parents who can make sufficient changes. The worry is that some will manage to keep these going over only a short time period. The next challenge is to try to ensure that changes are sustained in the longer term. We look at this in the next chapter.

Summary points

❏ Some parents have the potential to care for and nurture their children but practical and emotional pressures and preoccupations can get in the way. Family support can help some parents through a difficult period in their lives.

❏ Parents told us that the manner and approach that practitioners take towards them is important; they appreciate being shown respect and understanding, and practitioners being clear about their expectations.

❑ It may not be possible for busy practitioners to work with parents on all aspects of the support required, and so staff from other services may need to become involved. Even if the practitioner's role with the family is mainly a co-ordinating one, prioritising and spending time on some aspects of support may pay dividends in terms of relationship-building with parents.

❑ There are interesting ways of imparting knowledge and information about childcare to parents, which suit their particular style of learning. Some parents needed information reinforced, and reassurance that this was not unusual.

❑ Many parents talked about a lack of confidence in their parenting skills, particularly in managing children's behaviour if it was difficult; some were anxious about what other people thought of them and needed help to overcome this.

❑ Most parents found that parenting skills were best learnt through a 'hands-on' approach with support workers showing them how to do things and then doing them alongside them.

❑ Family support can be effective, but there needs to be clear signs of improved childcare skills within the child's timescales, particularly if the risks for the child are high.

CHAPTER 5

Building family resilience

'I have finished with everything and now I am on my own, after all the interventions – I just have to get on with it.' Parent, study G

Introduction

This chapter looks at family resilience, and how parents can be supported to develop it. Support from services can help parents to build confidence and skills in caring for their children, but this is usually provided over a period of only a few months. We often hear practitioners say that parents do well while supports are in place but that, once this ends, good intentions can slip and previous difficulties can re-emerge. Ongoing protective factors can be built so that the effects of the support will be more lasting, and parents can be helped to sustain the changes they have made.

In this chapter, we outline ways in which practitioners can contribute to the development of family resilience. Parents say that, once formal supports have ended, they feel they are more likely to retain their skills and confidence in parenting if some form of support 'scaffolding' is in place. Practitioners can encourage parents to develop coping strategies to deal with both practical problems and emotional hardships. They can help them become more confident in forging the informal supports and friendships that are an important aspect of being more resilient. We suggest potential 'domains' of family resilience and how this can be encouraged.

What is family resilience?

Children's resilience is a well-developed concept, and many practitioners take a resilience-based approach in their work with them. It is, arguably, just as important that those who support parents help them to develop their resilience also. Not only might this help parents cope with their own difficulties – if parents are resilient, they may be better placed to help their children become more resilient in turn. Children tend to base their ways of coping on what they have seen their parents do to manage their difficulties (Hill *et al.*, 2007). The idea of building family resilience, as a broader way of helping children build theirs, is now gaining ground. In Chapter 1, we outlined some aspects of a resilience-based approach, both in working with children and in encouraging parental and family resilience, and identified some similarities between them. Just as resilience-based work with children can be approached within key domains, parental and family resilience can be explored in similar ways.

Reflective exercise

Some of us are more resilient than others. How resilient do you think you are? What do you think has contributed to your degree of resilience? What do you think is helping you to develop your resilience further?

In describing what we see as the main aspects of parental resilience, we have drawn on what parents told us were helpful to them (a) in retaining what they had achieved through family support and (b) in building their coping skills to enable them to overcome difficulties after formal supports had ended.

It is important to remember that most of the parents who need support have faced, or are still facing, very challenging situations, often involving multiple problems. Some have encountered difficulties at various stages of their lives, sometimes with very little support. For some of us, it is by experiencing and overcoming adversity that we can become better equipped to cope with future problems. We may be able to build on the strengths we had to develop to get through difficult times to form a degree of resilience. Many of the parents who practitioners meet have struggled with, but managed to overcome, problems that would challenge even those of us who are well-supported. As one parent said to us:

> 'Come and try and live in our situation for a week.' Parent, study G

The following sections outline what we consider to be possible domains of family resilience and how parents can be supported to build them.

Feeling secure

> 'I was in a new home after I escaped domestic abuse and needed
> lots of practical help as the house was in a bad shape. The sup-
> port worker got grants for baby's clothing and decorating and
> got volunteers to paint the house. I always used to be worried
> about the baby and I didn't use to leave the house – but I do
> now.' Parent, study J

We described earlier what parents told us about how hard it was to feel
secure if you were living in poor accommodation and that, by supporting them to change or improve their environment, practitioners could
help them feel more motivated to care for their children in a more proactive way. We stressed that one of the keys aim of family support is to
help parents with their family's basic needs, such as decent, safe housing and adequate furniture. This was very important to parents and
cannot be over-emphasised. We saw that this was also a prerequisite
to undertaking support work with parents to put routines in place and
share enjoyable times with their children. If this sense of security can
be established in the long term, parents, like children, will have a firmer
basis on which to sustain the changes brought about through the family
support provided.

Family example: Kirsty

Kirsty and her children were living in poorly maintained and scantily furnished
accommodation, and she was suffering from depression; this was affecting
her care of the children. She said it would make her feel better if the garden
could be cleared of rubbish to make it a decent place for her children to
play. Her social worker arranged for this happen using Community Payback
service users. Pride in her garden and a good environment for the family
to be in, and for the children to play in, led to Kirsty deciding to tidy and
decorate the house. She started to feel more positive about herself and
her circumstances. This practical piece of work led to her feeling more
motivated to care for and play with her children, who also loved playing
outside.

If parents have been supported to communicate confidently with staff
at services such as housing, they will feel more able to approach them if
problems arise which need fixing: for example, house repairs and other
tenancy issues:

'The support staff did practical things with me, even helped me paint the living room, and put laminate floor down, it helped me have some pride in my space.' Parent, study J

Financial insecurity was a problem for many of the parents who talked to us. Part of the support offered to them was help in getting financial and benefits advice, and in budgeting and trying to avoid debt. While practitioners may not have been able to help them completely overcome financial insecurity, encouraging them to develop the skills and tools to continue (a) budgeting, (b) to feel able to deal with staff at agencies such as the Benefits Agency and (c) to ask for advice from agencies such as Citizens' Advice Bureaux, may enable them to keep their finances on a more even keel.

Some parents expressed strong views about the neighbourhoods in which they lived. Some found their housing estates unsafe and were worried about their children playing outside. Others, especially those who had lived in an area for a long time and knew many of the other families, had found ways to manage living in what was seen as an unsafe area. They preferred to continue living in these areas, even with their inadequacies, because they felt they 'belonged'. Indeed, some talked about how they could become involved in helping to improve their communities – an idea that we pick up again later in this chapter.

Good mental and physical health

'Building up my confidence has made a difference to my children. Because I'm more confident and happy and they can see that, it's had an effect on them.' Parent, study H

Many parents told us that, during the period in which they received support, they had experienced improved mental health – in some cases, this applied to both themselves and their children. Support had enabled them to seek help from GPs and other medical professionals, sometimes for quite serious mental health conditions. Support staff had suggested strategies and activities to try to counteract the effects of anxiety and depression, to foster greater self-confidence and to try to reduce feelings of powerlessness. Some parents had taken up advice and support about how to keep themselves and their children healthy (physically and mentally) by adopting a balanced diet, an active lifestyle and by getting into the habit of keeping dentist and doctor appointments.

Family example: James

James was eleven years old and lived with his parents in a high-rise block of flats. The family were very isolated, with no friends or family living nearby. Both parents were drug users. James' parents rarely ventured outside the family home. They lived on convenience food and fizzy drinks. James was overweight and bullied at school.

Support work took place to help James' parents understand the impact on James of their diet choices. Both parents agreed to participate with James in the Active Children Eating Smart (ACES) programme – a six-week plan that focused on active and healthy lifestyles. The family required a lot of encouragement from support staff to attend. As well as going along to the programme, the family were encouraged to get out and about, by walking in their local community, and to join the local community gym. Staff accompanied the family to gym sessions and supported them to participate in various activities. James enjoyed the programme and the gym, and began speaking to other children. His confidence grew, and he felt less anxious at school. James enjoyed a game of football with his friends and, having sustained the changes, his parents started to feel the benefits of a healthy lifestyle. This led to them looking at ways to reduce their drug use.

Several parents said they had put together a folder of the tips and information that support staff had used with them, and some said they regularly referred back to this. They were keen to keep up the habits and routines they had put in place while receiving support:

> 'I'm still trying to do some of the things I learnt. Sometimes I forget – you can't change overnight but it's happening slowly.' Parent, study B

Not surprisingly, parents said they felt more able to cope with caring for children if they felt happy and healthy, at least some of the time, although some were also wary when life was going well:

> 'We feel that we're almost too scared to be happy because it can all come crashing down.' Parent consultant, study F

Many of the parents had formed good relationships with the workers who were supporting them, and this, in itself, was an important factor in them feeling less depressed and anxious:

> 'Some social workers are good – often the student social workers who have more time to spend with us. When they go out of our lives we really miss them.' Parent consultant, study F

This makes it particularly important that, as this relationship ends, parents are not left feeling abandoned – ensuring that at least one ongoing supportive relationship is in place should be a key aim of family support work at as early a stage as possible. If parents are to build resilience and coping skills, they will need encouragement to persevere with the positive changes that they have achieved. A friend, family member, befriender or peer mentor who can provide (if possible, mutual) support to retain at least some achievable aspects of a healthy lifestyle was seen by parents as extremely helpful. This ties in with the next important strand of resilience-building which we describe below.

Social support networks (or having at least one good friend)

'The support workers made me less scared of meeting new people. I've met other mums who I can talk to about how hard it is to look after a baby, and we get tips from each other. That will help me go into the nursery when the time comes.' Parent, study J

Parents told us that an informal social network, even if it includes just one or two people, enables them to feel supported once formal help from professionals has come to an end. Having a social network or at least one good friend is considered to be a building block of resilience. Many family support services try to encourage parents to form or strengthen existing relationships, which can offer support on an ongoing basis. Group activities can be used to foster friendships; joint family activities can be arranged if two or more families seem to have formed a good relationship:

'In the summer holidays we met up with other parents and children and that was really fine. It would be good to have a social get-together every month – maybe cook a meal at the family centre or something. It doesn't matter to me if people know I come here for help.' Parent, study H

Family example: James and Lewis families

Carol James and Janice Lewis met during an open day at a family centre and their children, aged three, enjoyed playing together. They also both had one child under two. With support from centre staff, the two women decided to meet up at a local park, which has a café attached to it. They then decided that they would like to venture outside their local community, as the support they gave one another made them feel more confident about taking public transport and going somewhere new. They consulted centre staff about where they could take the children in the city, which would not be too expensive for their limited budgets. Parents and children enjoy one another's company and the opportunities to do new things.

As well as reducing social isolation and providing companionship, social networks can offer emotional and practical help, information and advice (Jack, 2000). If a good bond can be formed during the formal support period, this can continue afterwards as described by this father:

> 'If we're having trouble through the week we contact each other. If someone is having a bad day we can reach out to each other.' Parent, study P

Many parents remarked how helpful it was to know that yours is not the only family who is struggling:

> 'It took away the feeling of despair. I had felt terrible at times. We could encourage each other and say to each other that things will get better. It was good to talk about the difficulties and mull over the bad and good things that had happened to us.' Parent, study B

If shared interests are found, there is plenty of scope for developing useful and enjoyable activities, which can involve all the family:

> 'We started doing a couple of wee raised beds and one of the guys has really taken to it – he's set up his garden and he's growing his tatties and cabbage. It's really great for the kids as well, getting them growing things in the garden.' Parent, study P

This ties in with the notion of the chain effect of different aspects of resilience development (Gilligan, 2001b). For example, an anxious parent may feel more able to start taking their child to playgroup if they have a friend who is willing to go with them – once they start going along, their social network has the potential to grow from there.

Good communication

> 'My children and I are definitely getting on better. A lot of this
> is me trying not to react too strongly to things and talking it
> through calmly. I'm not screaming and shouting at them now.'
> Parent, study A

Parents told us that, being encouraged to talk to one another about what was going on in the family and to find calm and constructive ways to express their feelings, had been an important part of the family work they had undertaken. This included parents talking to one another and having a shared and consistent approach to children's behaviour. It also involved parents talking openly with their children about emotions and the good and difficult things going on within the family. Parents said it had also been helpful to develop skills in communicating with people outside the family, such as teachers and health staff.

As with the other skills that parents had learnt, it was important for practitioners to find ways to help them to continue with this in the longer term. The ability to talk things over within the family, and to do so in a calm and helpful way, are important aspects of family resilience. Practitioners often used role modelling of situations to teach communication skills, and parents said that this helped to make the skills 'stick':

> 'We learnt about giving children choices and getting them to
> help, like with shopping – I tried that in ASDA, gave my daugh-
> ter her own shopping list and she felt so pleased and confident
> like.' Parent, study D

The emotional literacy work, which some families had taken part in, had included exercises to promote good communication. Family-based emotional literacy is often approached in a structured way, and families are usually given materials that they can continue to use in the future. Some parents said that they referred back to their reading materials after the formal programme had ended. And remembering and replaying how prac-titioners had role-modelled good communication had also been helpful:

> 'I have seen differences; mainly as a result of the effect the group
> had on me – it caused me to react differently to my boys. Also
> the support I got from other parents and the group leaders, their
> supportive approach, has had a lasting effect.' Parent, study H

Family example: Jones family

The Jones family had taken part in a course of emotional literacy (EL) which involved playing board games, telling stories, artwork, role play and generally having fun together. They collected a portfolio of materials that recorded their work. When they found themselves having arguments or tempers starting to become frayed, one of them would say 'let's play an EL game' and they would try to sit down, be calm and think of a way that they could work things out. Sometimes, they got out their portfolio to remind themselves what they would done in the course and how it might help them now.

Parents described how hard it can be to put new ways of dealing with situations into practice, especially during a crisis when everyone in the family is feeling fraught. Some parents were very honest about the extent to which they had been able to sustain changes and about their lapses:

> 'We did a family agreement and said how we wanted things to be. We had rules, such as more fun, hugs, more listening and less shouting. We still have a copy of it on the board and, though some things have gone out the window, we are still doing some of them.' Parent, study B

Making use of opportunities – education, training and work

> 'I want to get back to work and through talking to my support worker I have been able to fill in a college application.' Parent, study D

Those who work with children to develop their resilience recognise the importance of them being able to make the most of education, and later training, opportunities. We know that, if children are helped to manage in the school environment and can learn and achieve to the best of their ability, the benefits of the school experience can be wider than education alone (Daniel and Wassell, 2002b). School can be an important place for children to learn to form relationships with peers and adults, develop a sense of self-belief and attain social as well as intellectual skills. Family support can help parents to recognise the importance of this, not just for their children but sometimes also for themselves. A family learning ethos, if it can be sustained, can be an important part of developing family resilience:

'My son didn't know how to interact with other children, he needed help to build his confidence. He needed to learn everything again. He had one-to-one sessions with staff focusing on his schoolwork and went to time-to-talk groups – he loved those groups. I felt bad because I made him come to the service all during the summer holidays he was doing schoolwork as well as other things, but it was good for him. I could see a change in him; he seemed much happier. Then I thought – do you know what, I like learning what he's learning, too, so we learnt together.' Parent, study D

Some parents told us that they wanted their children to have different lives from their own and to have opportunities that they themselves felt they did not have. Once they saw that their child was enjoying school, and doing well at particular subjects, they saw the positive affect this had on the child and their feeling of self-determination. Believing that you can have an influence on your future is an important component of resilience.

Family example: Chloe

Chloe suffered from depression and was anxious about her ability to help her daughter with her homework. Doing this was often stressful and usually ended in arguments. Chloe remembered feeling miserable at school and struggled academically, because of her hearing loss, and she felt the teachers did nothing to support her through this. Enjoyable learning activities, such as word searches and crosswords, were found for Chloe, and she developed an interest in learning, which she had not experienced at school. She wanted to eventually feel confident enough to apply for college.

Chloe worked with a literacy worker on her skills and knowledge so she could support her daughter at homework time without feeling stressed. She grew in confidence as the weeks went on and was delighted to be able to help her daughter with her homework. The sessions have visibly raised Chloe's self-esteem. She felt able to apply for a course at the local college, which will open up further opportunities.

Taking up training and employment opportunities may require childcare provision, and some parents needed support to put this in place. Most nurseries and Early Years centres now offer flexible childcare to parents or carers who are studying or working:

'From not being able to take my children to school to now looking for a small part-time job. I wouldn't have done it without
support, though.' Parent, study J

Taking part in community-based activities and groups

'With support, I have started going to my local parent-and-toddler group and have met a few new friends. My son has met a lot
of little friends too. If you know one other person going along,
you are more likely to go.' Parent, study K

Some parents told us that, having built up their social networks and
feeling more confident in themselves, they had become more proactive
and involved in groups organised within their local communities. Ventur-
ing out of the house had been a gradual process for some, but many had
felt more relaxed about taking part in local activities by the time the period
of formal supports had ended. For some, this meant joining local groups,
such as playgroups and other activity groups for children or exercise groups
for adults. Continuing this on a sustained basis had helped them to feel
they belonged in their community and had also had beneficial effects on
their feelings of well-being and confidence. Supporting people to take on
responsibilities and roles within their community can lead to them feeling
respected and valued (Holman *et al.*, 1999).

Building relationships in the wider community is part of the process of
building 'social capital', as we discussed in Chapter 1. This can lead to parents feeling more able and motivated to make changes in their local neighbourhood, which will benefit themselves and their children. This ties in
with the community resilience initiatives being developed by Angie Hart,
which we also mentioned in Chapter 1 (Hart and Aumann, 2017).

Practice example: The fathers' group

The fathers' group has involved the wider community through fundraising
(a sponsored bungee jump), by putting on a pantomime that challenged
male/female parent stereotypes and by holding events at which local and
national politicians were asked to answer questions. They also made a film
drama that was shown at a National Year of the Father event. The group
support worker commented:

'The profile increases when you have events – the bungee thing
was well covered in the local press. We guys were proactive in
the election campaign – grilling the politicians and getting one

of them fundraising who is now an MP. I can't oversell how much
the younger men in our group are doing'.

Parents we talked with for another study had been encouraged by hearing about the experience of other communities in trying to improve their local environment and facilities through initiatives such as community asset-building (Russell, 2009).

Practice example: COMMUNITY CHANGE

Parents at a family support project were inspired by a discussion with Sir Harry Burns, at the time chief medical officer for Scotland, who talked about community asset-building projects both locally and in other parts of the UK. He helped them think about what they would like to change in their communities and how they might start to bring this about. Parents talked about safer and greener play spaces for children, local activities for children and parents, clubs for young people, support for carers, peer support for parents and opportunities to take part in volunteer work.

Resilience and sustainability

Building family resilience is an ongoing process with no discernible endpoint. Many factors will influence how families cope with difficult situations. What we are suggesting in this chapter is that by building some of the aspects of resilience described in this chapter, parents and children may be better placed to cope.

However, parents said that, from time to time, they may need a 'top-up' of professional support and that this should be made available without them having to jump over numerous hurdles to get it. Some support services do encourage families who have received their help to keep in contact and feel able to drop by or pick up the phone to them. The use of texting and some forms of social media are ways in which parents can keep in touch with services and can also be used for peer support. While these can be useful forms of communication, they can also be misused and are not a substitute for face-to-face contact.

As one parent said:

'It would be good to have follow-up of some sort because if you're doing okay you get less support. But it can still be difficult so I'm sure I will need support as my son gets older.' Parent, study A

Summary points

❑ A short-term period of support from professionals may be only the start of a longer-term process of helping parents to care for their children in a safe and nurturing way; some parents know they will probably require future support, perhaps as children get older and present them with new challenges. Developing family resilience and coping skills may help parents to sustain the changes they have made as a result of receiving support.

❑ Family resilience is a developing area of work; it shares some of the same characteristics as resilience-based work with children and can have similar chain effects, with progress in one area having the potential for a spin-off for others.

❑ Feeling physically and emotionally secure, looking after family members' mental and physical health and developing good family communication skills are all aspects of increased family resilience.

❑ Having a support network, even one or two reliable friends, is the bedrock of increasing resilience, and parents clearly saw the benefits of forming strong and sustained friendships.

❑ Becoming confident enough to make use of opportunities, having a sense of self-efficacy and control over their lives and feeling part of, or even taking a role in, the local community, all contributed to increased sense of parental resilience. This, in turn, had the potential to help families develop greater resilience.

CHAPTER 6

Are we making a difference?

'We are putting the things we learn into practice – it makes life a lot easier at home.' Parent, study B

Introduction

In this chapter, we consider how practitioners can assess whether the support they are offering to families is making a difference to the lives of parents and their children. To some extent, practitioners will know from their own observations whether children are more nurtured, and parents and children may also be telling them that family life has improved. However, professionals are now required to measure the effectiveness of their involvement in more formal ways by providing evidence of improved 'outcomes', especially for children. We discuss why this is important and make suggestions about how this might be done using methods which parents said made sense to them. We also describe some of the difficulties in looking at outcomes and effectiveness.

The main reason for providing support for families with children is to make life better for those children. Although children's views are not the focus of this book, we thought that this chapter would be a good place to include some of what the children and young people involved in our research studies said to us, which is relevant to this topic. While children were not thinking about 'outcomes' at such, they told us what they thought parents and carers needed to provide for them, in order to keep them healthy and happy, and about their experiences of talking to and receiving help from the support workers involved with themselves and their families.

Why should we measure effectiveness?

In our view there are three main reasons why practitioners should try to assess the effects on families of the support that is being provided to them. The first is for the benefit of:

- **individual families**: to measure whether family support is contributing to children's safety, health and well-being and to parents' ability to provide nurturing care for them. It enables practitioners to review the support being provided and continue, change or bring it to an end if another course of action is required, according to what they conclude.

Practitioners should constantly ask themselves how things are going with a family. A structured way of recording progress towards the desired 'outcomes' for a family, and involving family members in this, can be a helpful aid in looking at the detail of any changes. It can act as a tool for reflective practice in examining what worked well with a family in a particular situation. It also provides a structured way of recording evidence of the effectiveness (or not) of the support offered, in case this is required at a later date: for example, if legal proceedings for a statutory order become necessary.

The two other reasons for assessments are to assist with:

- **practice development**: to learn more about what types of support and approaches to it are most effective in helping parents and children, in order to inform the development of services in the future;
- **managerial and planning purposes**: to provide evidence about what types of support are effective when planning the (preferably) long-term funding of services.

What are the challenges in assessing the impact of family support?

Many evaluations of support services have, in the past, relied heavily on subjective feedback from parents and their own staff as evidence that the support provided has 'made a difference' to parents and their families. Most now recognise that this, by itself, does not constitute convincing evidence of the impact of the support, in particular on the safety and welfare of the children in the family. Much work has been undertaken to find meaningful ways to measure and record the effectiveness of family support, and a wide range of 'outcomes frameworks' have been, or are being, developed to help services to approach this.

Many services now make use of these structured 'outcomes' frameworks, which include lists of 'outcomes' and outcome indicators and various ways of measuring the extent to which individual families are meeting identified outcomes. A framework template is usually completed for each family using summarised descriptions of what has been achieved in relation to each desired outcome; some also use numerical scales to represent progress (or lack of it). Some services, including local authority social work services, education and health trusts, now aim to provide support in an integrated way, and staff from all the services involved with the family may contribute to the completion of the framework. In some organisations, 'results' are aggregated by some method to provide evidence of wider service 'outcomes'.

There are inherent challenges in devising outcomes-based approaches which truly reflect the complexities of people's lives and the effects on them of interventions, including that of family support. Our lives are subject to constant change and unpredictable events, and 'outcomes' are not static or final. There is probably no one method which does the job perfectly, and when we use outcomes frameworks we do so with their limitations in mind.

One option which is sometimes considered is that known as the realist approach to evaluation; it was developed by Kazi (2003) and followed on from the work of Pawson and Tilley (2007). This approach aims to explore what works for whom and in what circumstances and, given the individual nature of families and their situations, might offer a solution. Work is being undertaken to develop this approach in various settings across the UK: for example, as a way of looking at early intervention services for families in Scotland (Coles et al., 2015). Coles et al. have developed a protocol using realist methodology to develop a programme theory and use this to explore which types of interventions do or do not work for families in particular contexts.

The problem with 'outcomes'

Identifying outcomes and the extent to which they have been met is now part of the process of trying to measure whether children's lives have improved (or not) and assessing whether the intervention(s) provided have had an effect on them and their families. However, the term 'outcome' is not straightforward in itself and is often used in different ways. In their international review of parenting support evidence, Moran et al. (2004) discuss some of the difficulties with its use. They describe an 'outcome' as being something that has come about as a consequence of something else. They say that this cause-and-effect relationship means that outcomes can be influenced, for example, by offering a service which helps to improve a person's circumstances or to withstand stress in times of difficulty. An outcome has a sense of being an end product, and Moran *et al.* consider that this sets the bar high in relation to support services, as some outcomes may be reached slowly over a long period of time and may not always be in a positive direction – there can be setbacks within periods of progress.

In setting outcomes, it may be more realistic to set a relative one, such as the child being 'safer' and 'healthier', rather than the absolute ones of 'safe' and 'healthy', although this raises the question of how we know whether they are safe and healthy enough.

'Outcome indicators' are often used to break down broad outcomes and to describe more specific aims, usually tailored to individual children or families. These indicators may contribute to the achievement of the broad outcome or used as a way of 'indicating' that progress is being made towards meeting the outcome. However, the term 'indicators' is also sometimes employed, rather confusingly, to describe the actions or steps required to meet the desired outcomes. Clear thinking is needed when designing an outcomes framework to separate out actions from indicators and ensure that they are not used interchangeably.

As family support is usually provided on a short-term basis only, there is now a tendency to refer to 'progress towards an outcome' or to report on the 'direction of travel' towards an identified outcome. When a period of support comes to an end, even if a (realistic) outcome has been met or there is good progress towards it, it will be difficult to predict whether the improvements made can be sustained in the longer term, particularly after formal supports are withdrawn. If the family come to the attention of helping services at some point in the future, it will be possible to see what changes have not been maintained, and the reasons for this. If they do not, practitioners will not know if the supports they provided have resulted in greatly improved circumstances for the family, or whether they are struggling on but staying just below the radar of services.

When measuring the impact of family support, there is an added complication. While some of the work may be with children themselves, the main focus is likely to be on supporting parents to achieve positive outcomes for their children. Therefore, arguably, it may be necessary to identify desired outcome indicators, or aims, for both children and parents. Moran *et al.* (2004, p. 22) ask to what extent we should identify outcomes for parents as carers of children or as people in their own right, given that 'unless parents are functional as people, they are unlikely to be functional as care-givers'. Whatever the outcomes and outcome indicators identified for parents, there will certainly be actions which both practitioners and parents need to undertake to meet, or 'make progress towards', the outcomes identified for the children. These then need to be married together when reviewing how the support is going.

Reflective exercise

As professionals, we spend time thinking about the desired 'outcomes' for the parents and children we work with. Do you think in these terms in relation to yourself? What would you set as outcomes for yourself, your children or other family members? Are you making progress towards them, do you think? What are the factors which influence your ability to meet your aims and outcomes?

Other challenges in assessing and reporting impact

When evaluating services we cannot say with any certainty that the support offered, by itself, has led directly to the improvement in families' circumstances. People are usually subject to many influences in their lives, and the support provided may be just one factor – direct attribution is not realistic (Trinder, 2000). The most we can say is that it may, or is likely to, have contributed to changes. Having said that, it may be possible to make some cause-and-effect-type links: for example, if a practitioner has helped a family to move to better accommodation and other positive effects have stemmed from this.

In measuring and evidencing change, it is best if we can draw on the views of a wide range of people involved with the family. Parents often say that the support offered has 'made life better for them', and this is sometimes backed up by those practitioners providing the support. However, obtaining the views of third parties such as teachers, nursery staff and health professionals about the effects on children themselves will carry more weight in reporting progress (or lack of it). The move towards multi-agency collaboration in providing family support should enable this type of information to be gathered. Using an outcomes framework to structure these comments can be helpful.

There are challenges in reporting and writing up the ways in which family support has affected changes and improved outcomes for children (or not). Bringing together the various materials which practitioners have gathered, and providing a useful analysis of them to form some conclusions, are skilled tasks. It is helpful to include sufficient detail so that information about the effectiveness of support can be set in context while, at the same time, being concise and to the point. Most agencies have templates and formats for doing this, but many practitioners find it hard to achieve a good balance between sufficient detail and relevance.

Some frameworks make use of a number-based scaling system to record progress towards outcomes, and this is often aggregated, in some way, to try to evidence the effectiveness of services. Used on its own, this is overly simplistic, but it can be helpful in offering an overall guide to parents' 'direction of travel' in responding to the supports offered.

Some parents told us that they found number-based scales useful:

> 'It's helpful to have numbers in some ways so you can see how much you've done in so many months. It makes it clearer how to get from one number to the other.' Parent, study L

However progress and outcomes information is presented, it must be written in a way that makes sense to parents – and, if possible, to children and young people, too. It should be phrased sensitively while not omitting any important information, such as any identified risks for children and also for parents, if this affects their care of their children:

> 'I'm dyslexic so I can struggle to understand big words. Sometimes the language used is hard to understand – the words are long. Some people explain them, others don't.' Parent, study G

What might be included when measuring impact?

In order to try to assess the effectiveness of family support in meeting identified outcomes for individual families, we suggest that practitioners draw on a range of evidence types, if possible including those listed below which were used in the service identified in Study D:

- the views of parents about their experiences of the support – in what ways it was useful and any effects it had on them and their children;
- children's perspectives on whether theirs and their family's lives have changed while receiving the support;

- written views of staff from other agencies involved with family: for example, health visitors and teachers, as well as those of main practitioners providing support;
- an outcomes framework, the content of which is completed together with parents, which outlines:

  (a) the aims of the support (for both parents and children);

  (b) the desired short- and longer-term outcomes (with indicators to show how these are being met);

  (c) what needs to be done to achieve them;

  (d) and charts any progress made towards the aims or reasons why this has not happened; this uses all available evidence including the results of any standardised measures or customised scales and any visual tools. (Parents, children, support staff and staff from other agencies can contribute to this.)

In Figure 6.1, we describe the methods used in that service (Study D).

Figure 6.1: A model for outcomes measurement

Evidence type	Method of obtaining evidence	Contributors
Information for completion of outcomes framework	Use of visual tools such as the Outcomes Star (a), the Well-being Web (b), completion of SDQs (c) and PDH questionnaires (d) and/or customised forms to chart the actions completed to reach the desired aims	Parents, children, family support staff and other professionals, including twice-yearly SDQ completion by parents and teachers
Views of parents about experience of receiving the support	Semi-structured individual interviews and discussion groups, preferably led by someone not involved in providing direct support	Parents and possibly other family members and friends
Views of children	Child-friendly tools to help children look at any changes in their lives	Children
Practitioner views	Written descriptive information, using a concise template or form	Family support staff and from other services involved with family

Key to Figure 6.1

(a) The Outcomes Star is a family of tools which consists of a number of scales arranged in the shape of a star. There are descriptions of each point of the scale, and the practitioner and family member use these to complete the star to identify progress towards individual outcomes. These can later be reviewed, and changes in score plotted. Available from URL: www.outcomesstar.org.uk (accessed 6 January 2018)

(b) The Well-being Web was developed by practitioners in Angus, Scotland as a diagrammatic way to capture progress towards outcomes for children and adults. Its principles are similar to those of the Outcomes Star. Available from URL: http://lx.iriss.org.uk/content/girfec-wellbeing-web (accessed 19 January 2018)

(c) The Goodman Strengths and Difficulties Questionnaire (SDQ) is a validated tool that scores children's behaviour, including their peer relationships and pro-social behaviour, over a period of time and can be completed by parents, teachers and older children. It is widely used in the UK by practitioners and research-ers. Available from URL: www.sdqinfo.org (accessed 6 January 2018)

(d) The Parenting Daily Hassles (PDH) questionnaire is a validated tool that measures the impact and frequency of twenty potential parenting hassles. Many parents who have used it say they can relate well to the experiences it describes. Available from URL: www.socialworkerstoolbox.com/the-parenting-daily-hassle-scale (accessed 6 January 2018)

This descriptive and numerical information can be brought together, using the outcomes framework as a structure, to give a picture of the extent to which progress is being made towards identified outcomes for both parents and children.

Example of a family outcomes framework

This is a concise version of a completed outcomes framework. In practice, it would be more detailed – this offers 'headline' suggestions of what might be included.

The McCloud family

Paula and Keith live with their children, Jason (ten years old) and Andrew (aged eight). Keith is the boys' stepfather. Both parents use drugs and alcohol, and Paula suffers with anxiety and depression, for which she has prescription drugs. Andrew is being bullied at school, and neither of the boys attends school regularly. Jason does much of the caring for Andrew, and often has to organise the shopping and meals for the family. The family are isolated with no extended family nearby.

Outcomes and indicators (to be explained in more detail in parent and child-friendly language)

Outcomes: Children	Indicators (how we will recognise change)
Safer, with parents taking responsibility for them	Keith and Paula showing care of the boys; also doing the shopping, cooking, washing and cleaning; drug and alcohol use reduced, parents' aware of and mini-mising risks for boys
Improved emotional and physical health and ability to express feelings	Jason and Andrew feeling able to talk with support worker about worries; appointments kept with GP and dentist; parents and children talking more about who does what in family
Improved school attendance	Self-explanatory (check with school)
Coping with and enjoying school	Children's, parents' and teachers' views of how school is going for the boys. Are they learning? Are they mixing with peers? Are they happy?

More support and social activities, especially with friends	Both boys have someone they can go to for help and one activity they attend regularly
Improved confidence and self-esteem	Examples from the boys' parents, support staff and teachers or from the boys themselves that show that they feel more confident and proud of their achievements
Outcomes: parents	Indicators (how we will recognise change)
Reduced substance use	Paula and Keith attending drug and alcohol services and showing evidence of reduced use
Greater knowledge of children's needs	Keith and Paula talking about child development with support worker; showing understanding of effects of their drug/alcohol use, what both boys need from them and what to expect from Jason
Increased confidence in parenting	Keith and Paula able to show that they have confidence/motivation to parent
More skilled in caring for children and providing for their needs	Keith and Paula spending time with boys, cooking meals, taking them out, being up in the morning to get them organised for school
Able to encourage children's learning	Keith and Paula having regular contact with boys' class teachers; helping with homework
Wider social and emotional support	Both parents involved with one support or activity group (as a start)

Aims of the children and their parents

○ **Jason**: to have friends to go out to the skate park with; not to have to shop and cook and look after Andrew; to have a happy mother; to get on better with Keith;

○ **Andrew**: to have friends and go to school; to go out sometimes with my family; not to be told what to do by Jason; to have better clothes and not have all the money spent on drink and drugs;

○ **Paula**: to feel better about going outside the house; to have a friend to talk to; for the boys to go to school and Andrew not get bullied; to get a part-time job;

○ **Keith**: to get out of debt and not spend so much money on drugs; to have a holiday; to get on better with the boys and spend more time with them.

Actions

These would usually be outlined in relation to each of the indicators above and contain more detail. In summary, this might include Keith and Paula being supported by the worker to attend drug and alcohol services, to meet with the boys' teachers to discuss support for them in school and to arrange dental and possibly GP appointments for the boys, if there were current health problems. Other actions could include the support worker arranging sessions with Keith and Paula about children's care needs at different stages and about developing their parenting skills, in particular minimising risks for the boys resulting from their drug and alcohol use; this would be followed by sessions with the whole family after school to see what had changed and try out some activities together. Another action could be for the support worker to help Paula to find a local group she would like to attend and support her to join it.

For the boys, the support worker's actions would include keeping in touch with the school about the boys' attendance and progress in mixing with other children and also meeting the boys separately to see how things are for them and arrange activities for Andrew. Jason would be helped to get more involved in skate boarding or to go to activities with other children his age.

Evidence

○ The school staff and drugs and alcohol service staff can provide some factual information (e.g. about attendance) to evidence any progress with some of the outcome indicators.

○ Visual tools, such as the Outcomes Star, might be used with both parents and boys to look at any changes and then written up to demonstrate evidence.

○ Validated scales such as SDQ could be completed by boys, parents and possibly teachers; the parents might find the PDH questionnaire useful.

○ Concrete examples provided by the boys, parents, support staff and other professionals involved with the family included for each indicator, backed up by information from the scales and visual tools, where available.

Analysis and conclusions

There will be descriptive text in relation to each outcome indicator, which demonstrates any progress made in each area, together with contextual explanations about why this did not take place. There should also be a summary and analysis of what this means for the family, particularly in relation to the boys' safety and well-being, and how their parents have been able to demonstrate their willingness and ability to change (or not) and make progress towards meeting the identified outcomes and indicators. Future support needs and plans, as well as some outcome indicators, may need amending, after consultation with the family and other professionals.

Children's views about the aims of family support

> 'Some social workers asked our parents what they wanted but they didn't ask us.' Young person consultant, study F

Although the focus of this book is on what parents told us, we thought that this section on children's 'outcomes' would benefit from a brief look at children's own views about this. Practitioners are aware of the importance of gathering children's and young people's views during assessments and reviews of their care, and creative and meaningful ways of doing this are being tried across the country, including the use of Viewpoint (www.vpthub.com; accessed 19 January 2018). This is an online consultation tool now employed by many social work and social care services across the UK and in Australia and Canada. Audio Computer-Assisted Self-Interviewing (ACASI) enables children and young people to put across their views in a user-friendly medium. Similarly, researchers are finding new ways of involving children in their studies to enable them to give their views about the services they receive and also as active participants in undertaking research (Brownlie *et al.*, 2006; McCabe and Horsley, 2008; Wilson and Milne, 2013).

It has been suggested that not enough attention has been paid to children's views of what makes a good parent, and how parenting support could help parents with this (Moran *et al.*, 2004). When asked, children are likely to talk mainly about their day-to-day family lives than about how the care their parents are giving them may shape their future 'outcomes'. However, many have insights into the possible longer-term consequences of some of the gaps in their parenting (Burgess *et al.*, 2014).

Figure 6.2: What children say they need from their parents and carers (Burgess *et al.*, 2014)

Very important	A house, health, food, clothes, safety, love and help with school
Important	Money, friends, pets, praise, cuddles, fresh air (this last one from the 6–11 year olds, not the over twelves)
Quite important	Toys, sleeping, going to the doctor and dentist (from the 6–11 year olds only); Not moving house a lot, attention, consistent adults (over twelves)

The children and young people who talked with us for our neglect research said that staying healthy, doing well at school, having friends and feeling good about themselves were important to them, and, in this respect, their hopes and aspirations were similar to what adults wished for them. They wanted parents to spend more time with them and give them more attention. Many understood why their parents were unable to care for them:

> 'It would have been better if my mum could have kept us but, if you've had a hard past, you think it's okay to look after kids that way.' Young person, study G

While some young people talked about the ways that professionals might be able to help their parents to change, so that they could look after them, others thought that the type of family support they received was not helpful in improving their situation:

> 'Some of us had family support workers and some of them could have helped our family more. For example, some of us played a game where you pick up a card with an emotion on it and then we had to tell our parents how we felt in certain situations or how they made us feel. Then when the family support worker left, we had big family arguments about it. So it's not a good idea to open up feelings and then just leave – everyone shouts at each other and then we're all upset. Some of us had family support for years and years, and it didn't really help us much. Please respect our views if we don't want to have this sort of help.' Young people consultant, study F

> 'Some parents you just can't help.' Young people consultant, study F

Young people told us what would help them talk to adults about difficulties at home when parents were unable to care for them. They said that:
- Adults need to be aware of the signs that children were unhappy and act on them:

> 'I think it's the adults who need to approach children if they think something's not right, it's not up to the children to approach them. It can be a big burden for a child to ask for help.' Young person, study G

- Professionals need to make it possible for children to talk about what is important to them, while understanding why this was hard:

    'My teacher realised [that things weren't good at home] but I think she was worried about asking me. They need more training and need to have time to ask children what's going on at home. I would have told her if she'd asked me. But she was kind to me, all the same.' Young person, study G

- Professionals need to be clear with children about how they might be able to help them and their families:

    'We need to have people's jobs explained to us. Who are they? What is their role? Why and how might they help us?' Young person, study G

- Once involved with the child's family, professionals should try to make a good relationship with the children, as well as with their parents:

    'The social worker was good at asking me in careful ways how things were at home and if I was comfy there. I could open up more when I was out of the house, when we went out to do things like activities. It's harder to talk in places where wrong things have happened.' Young person, study G

Some children told us that they took part in separate activities, which were designed to run alongside the support being offered to their parents. These often took place in schools, sometimes led by school staff or by family support workers who came into school. However, some young people thought that family support might usefully include children doing things together with parents, as a way of bringing families together:

    'What would be even better would be to get the dad to join in, too. Find something they all enjoy and put him at ease first. If the dad and son had that connection, spending an hour a day with that kid could mean the world to him – some dads just don't realise how much it'd mean to that kid.' Young person, study G

In looking to the future and in thinking about their own personal aims, some young people said they would learn from their experiences of being parented and try to do things differently so that they could be better parents to their own children.

Summary points

❏ Assessing change in children's and families' situations during and after the period of family support is important; it can also help practitioners and managers to gauge the effectiveness of the services provided for families and, in so doing, inform future practice developments.

❏ It is difficult to measure the impact of family support as many other factors are likely to influence parents' ability to care for their children; we may be able to say that it played a part, perhaps a significant part, in helping children and parents.

❏ Outcomes Frameworks can be a useful way of assessing progress towards the aims identified for and by the family. The use of the term 'outcomes' should be clear and not confused with 'actions'.

❏ Visual 'tools' can be employed to gather the views of children, parents and practitioners and used to write concise descriptions and analysis of progress (or lack of it) towards outcomes; standardised measures and scales can also be undertaken to provide more evidence. The completed framework form must be backed up by facts and examples, and make sense to parents, even if they do not agree with everything it says.

❏ Children and young people could be insightful when describing what parents needed to do for them, both on an everyday basis and to improve their life chances – they could also understand why some parents found this hard. The main message for professionals was to take the initiative in asking children if they needed help and to be clear about what sort of help they could give them.

CHAPTER 7

Conclusion

We hope that hearing what parents told us about the support they had received and what was helpful for themselves and their families has been useful. Our intention in writing this book was to enable practitioners from all disciplines to reflect on what parents said and to consider making use of this, where possible, in their practice. We are keenly aware that the views of others are also important: for example, those of the children and young people in the family, and of practitioners themselves. We know that some parents are so preoccupied by their own circumstances and problems that they lose sight of what is best for their children. Some may not manage to care for them, even with intensive help. But many can be supported to do so, and we believe that their perspectives are an important part of planning this support.

In thinking about practitioners' work with families, we were struck by the fact that many of the areas we cover are applicable to the practitioners who are providing the support, as well as to the parents themselves. In supporting parents to enhance their knowledge, confidence and skills, practitioners in their turn need to be equipped with each of these or at least the means to develop them. In her review of child protection, Munro (2011, p. 84) talks about the need for social workers' knowledge and skills to be 'radically improved from initial training through to continuing professional development'. She writes, among other things, about the importance of the development of relationship-building skills and communication, of gaining increased knowledge and expertise in giving evidence in court and in keeping up to date with the latest research into practice developments.

Supporting families can be a demanding and emotional task and practitioners need to feel nurtured, valued and supported when undertaking it. We would agree with Munro's (2011) conclusion that we are more likely to be able to help others if we feel supported ourselves. Practitioners' own resilience may be tested in the process of undertaking this work, and they may need to find ways to bolster this themselves, at the same time as helping families to do likewise. When we start to think about it, we can see how being the 'supported' and the 'supporter' mirror one another in a number of ways.

How can practitioners increase their knowledge, confidence and skills?

Knowledge

Practitioners are learning all the time as they go about their day-to-day work with families. They learn from listening to and watching their colleagues, from the words and reactions of the families they work with and through their contact with professionals from other disciplines. An important prerequisite to this learning is to have an open mind and to be prepared to be challenged about what you understand to be correct, or thought you knew, both directly and indirectly – accepting that the views of others can be as valid as your own.

It is hard to find the time to read research and practice materials when you are a busy and, quite possibly, tired and stressed practitioner. Some organisations produce briefing materials, which summarise the latest research and practice evidence, making them easier to digest than some academic studies (e.g. Research in Practice; IRISS; Social Care Institute for Excellence/SCIE; National Children's Bureau). They can provide a good guide to further reading if practitioners have an interest in a particular area of work.

Most practitioners have opportunities to take part in training courses, as part of their continuing professional development or as required by the needs of their service. While these can vary in quality, at the very least, if they offer opportunities for practitioners to share and discuss ideas about practice, they can be invaluable, and the best ones can act as an inspiration to world-weary professionals who need a day away from the pressures of direct front-line work. Even a few simple practice tips can help to inspire new enthusiasm.

There is also a mass of Internet-based resources, which, if used with care and discretion to ensure that sites are reliable, can be a source of ideas and information about practice in the field of parenting, child care and child development: for example, the social worker's toolbox (available from URL: www.socialworkerstoolbox.com/category/parenting; accessed 6

January 2018) and the 'Oxford Research Encyclopedia' (online; available from URL: http://oxfordre.com; accessed 6 January 2018).

Confidence

Starting out as a newly qualified practitioner can be difficult, and it takes time to feel confident and relatively assured that work with families and their children is helpful and safe. Confidence primarily comes with experience; every family's circumstances are different, and the varied situations that practitioners encounter will help them build a bank of experience. However, even very experienced practitioners can have their confidence shaken if a particularly difficult situation arises with a family. When this occurs, practitioners often question their judgement, and it is crucial that there are colleagues with whom they can talk this over.

It is important for practitioners to remember those pieces of work that go well, however small, as well as those that do not work out as planned. Expectations of families must be realistic – if they are, changes for the better will be more likely. If practitioners show some degree of confidence in what they are doing, this will, in turn, enable parents to have confidence in them. This confidence must be based on 'grounded' or evidence-based practice, that is practice which is tried and tested.

One of the keys to confidence building, as well as rebuilding, is to have someone who practitioners can talk their practice over with and, if appropriate, reaffirm their actions and the reasoning behind them. Good supervision from a competent manager is the best option, where possible, but, in the absence of this, peer support from colleagues, particularly experienced ones, can also be invaluable. Talking ideas over with colleagues is a vital part of good teamwork and can bolster the confidence of the whole team, through the development of a culture that encourages shared learning.

Skills

We have all met skilled practitioners who can combine a sensitive, empathic approach to parents with the firmness and authority which, at times, is also required. Practitioners' own personality traits play a large part in their ability to relate to people, and their skills are then honed through life and work experience. So to what extent can the skills and attributes required to be an effective practitioner really be learnt? We contend that, to some degree, these 'soft' skills can be developed through spending time with skilled colleagues and taking note of how they approach and relate to the families with whom they work.

Shadowing others in their direct work with families, observing the language they use and how they frame sensitive topics, taking note of how they prepare for their visits, learning tips about how to approach different situations are all useful ways of building skills. In effect, learning from role modelling by colleagues, in the same way that parents found helpful when they were learning skills from practitioners about how to manage children's behaviour.

How can practitioners be nurtured and how can they build their resilience?

In an earlier chapter, we heard from parents of the importance of feeling nurtured so that they would know how to be nurturing to their children. In many respects, practitioners also need to feel nurtured so that they, in turn, can call on their inner reserves to encourage parents in their own caring role. Ideally, a nurturing employer is one who provides a conducive working environment, who values and praises good practice and may even come up with some rewards and comforts to ease the passage of the working week: for example, time for coffee breaks and team lunches. In the absence of this, especially with the drive towards 'hot-desking' and open-plan offices, practitioners may need to look to colleagues for small but important nurturing gestures, which make working life more manageable.

It has been suggested that 'an inexperienced and unstable workforce leaves children and their families vulnerable to ineffective and potentially damaging interventions' (Gibbs, 2009). Gibbs stresses the importance of staff feeling valued, being given support in their work, having a sense of self-efficacy and undertaking reflective practice. In their *Resource Guide for Child Protection Managers*, Gibbs *et al.* (2009) refer to a six-factor model developed by Tony Morrison, which demonstrates the 'chain of influence' between supervision provided to practitioners and outcomes for children and families (Morrison, 2005). These factors are role clarity; role security; emotional intelligence and empathy; observation and assessment; appropriate partnership; and power and planning. Gibbs *et al.* (2009) then apply this model more broadly to other leadership processes and wider levels of management. They suggest that what happens between staff at different levels makes its way through the chain to the practitioner–client relationship.

In some respects, a nurtured workforce goes hand-in-hand with one that is resilient. Building resilience in the workforce in general, and in individual staff members in particular, has benefits for everyone, including management and the families who are receiving services. If practitioners feel secure in their employment, healthy, have good support networks and the chance to learn and develop, they will probably have less sickness absence and stay in their post for longer periods of time. It has been suggested that a service may be of higher quality if staffed by a robust and resilient workforce who feel secure in their employment, have good self-esteem as a result of their work being valued and who believe in the efficacy of the work they are doing (Antcliff, 2010).

Future practice developments

As we have seen, family support encompasses a range of practices designed to help parents and carers look after their children by providing emotional, social and practical support and assisting with the development of parenting skills. Practice in this area is constantly evolving as we learn more about what is most effective for parents and children. The capacity to put these developments into practice is largely dependent on the commitment of political leaders to adequately fund services to provide help for all the families who require it. Policy developments take place constantly, and we thought we would end our book with a look at a policy development that could be of significant influence in the future direction of family support.

Self-directed support

Self-directed support (SDS) is a major policy development across the UK and stems from the work of 'In Control', an organisation established in 2003 by a group of carers for people with disabilities. Its aim is to transform social care services by enabling families to make use of personalised budgets as a way of taking charge of their support. The principles have attracted much political support, and the approach is in the process of being piloted across the UK for use with a range of 'service users'. It has many advocates among practitioners and 'service users' alike, but is not without its critics, who have identified strengths and weaknesses in the policy and suggest that it may not meet the ambitions many had hoped for, particularly if financial resources continue to be stretched (Slasberg *et al.*, 2012).

In 2007, the Children's Programme was set up to develop the use of SDS for a range of families with children and young people who are involved with services. 'In Control' has since worked with more than forty children's services in England and Wales, and some of the learning and experiences from the initiatives developed within this programme are available (Crosby *et al.*, 2012). These include the use of SDS in tandem with a Signs of Safety approach, as well as examples of it being employed at an early intervention stage of family support (Crosby and Wheeler, 2010; Keilty, 2014). In Northern Ireland, Health and Social Care Trusts have been developing the use of SDS over the last five years, primarily for adults and children with disabilities and their families.

The Scottish government has taken a step further and enshrined the SDS approach in legislation, saying it is committed to 'driving a cultural shift around the delivery of care and support in Scotland, with self-directed support becoming the mainstream approach' (Scottish Government, 2010). The Social Care (Self-directed Support) (Scotland) Act 2013 and associated guidance outline the new duties placed on local authorities and the principles underpinning its use. The more recent Children and Young People (Scotland) Act 2016 legislation has widened this provision. Implementation of the national SDS strategy (Scottish Government, 2010) requires local authorities to consider how the SDS agenda can be integrated with GIRFEC, including how it might help improve the transition to adult services for young people. It has made funds available to all Scottish local authorities to pilot ways in which SDS might be used within services for children.

In many ways, the principles of an SDS approach, with its emphasis on increased self-determination for families and more of a partnership relationship between them and the professionals they are involved with, fit well with some of the messages from parents relayed in this book. An empowering approach, which gives them greater say in the nature of the support they need and a more equal relationship with professionals, could, for example, be beneficial in boosting parents' confidence and feelings of self-efficacy. The individual nature of families' circumstances would seem to fit well with a personalised-type approach to identifying and meeting their needs.

It also ties in with the current developments to encourage 'co-production' – defined by SCIE as 'people who use services and carers working with professionals in equal partnerships towards shared goals' (SCIE, 2015). In the statutory guidance to the Care Act 2014 in England and Wales, co-production is considered a key part of implementing the Act.

There are a growing number of examples of how this is now being used in practice across the UK (SCIE, 2015). In Scotland, the co-production principle was an integral part of the Public Social Partnerships (PSP), led by third-sector agencies and funded by the (Scottish) government (Scottish Government, 2011). A number of PSP projects were set up in 2013 to support families who were 'just coping', some of which involved families in designing services and having a role in recruiting staff (Burgess *et al.*, 2015a).

While we can see potential benefits of some aspects of an SDS approach in some circumstances, SDS also throws up a number of challenges, which will need to be worked through carefully by those implementing it at a local level. A small research study for one Scottish local authority undertaken in 2015 identified some potential benefits and challenges in an SDS approach piloted by its staff (Burgess, 2015). Ambitiously, they decided to use it with families whose support needs fell within a spectrum from early stage intervention to families with a child on the Child Protection Register and who were involved with social work, health and/or targeted educational support. As part of the approach, the intention was to hold a Family Network Meeting, similar to Family Group Conferencing (Ashley and Nixon, 2007), involving all close family members and friends of the child in planning, and possibly contributing to, the required help identified. Outcomes for children would be set using the locally devised Measuring Progress framework.

The intention had been to consult with families and children to ask their views about the approach, although this proved impossible because of low take-up during the period of the study. However, some interesting points were made by social workers and other professionals who had started to think about and use the approach.

Professionals thought that SDS had the potential to reinvigorate 'relationship-based' work with families. Helping a family with practical improvements to their lives, using a small SDS budget, was seen as a way of building a more co-operative relationship with families, some of whom view social workers, in particular, in a negative light. Small but important changes, such as improvements to the families' home, could have a spin-off effect:

> 'Some small changes can be a catalyst to confidence-building, reduced depression and families getting closer. It may not lead to magical overnight changes and it may involve some risks but it may be worth trying.' Social worker, study N

Most thought that using SDS could promote greater creativity in their interventions with families, and that jointly agreed actions could lead more directly to clearly identified outcomes. This might help build trust between practitioners and families and make any difficult conversations that might be required more acceptable to parents. For some practitioners, the SDS way of working was a development of what they were already doing, with the added element of sharing budget decisions with families, rather than adopting a whole new approach to their work.

The main challenges identified by practitioners were in applying an SDS approach in situations where professionals and parents or carers were not in agreement about a child's needs. Where there was conflict or lack of trust between the two groups, the notion of empowering parents or carers to direct their own support seemed out of place:

> 'SDS can be hard for social workers to grasp when working with families where there are children at risk and there may be conflict with the family. There may be issues about who is in control and who has authority, and SDS might be seen as giving into the demands of parents. There would need to be clarity about how the children's needs are being met in this case.' Social worker, study N

For social workers in particular, this brought into sharp focus the competing demands of their role in some circumstances, in relation to authoritative practice and balancing this with families' self-determination – the tensions between care and control and how to manage these in their work with families.

There were also practical considerations such as families needing to be aware of the support options available to them and realistic expectations about what could be provided. Different service commissioning arrangements to meet the demand of family-identified needs might be required. Practitioners who had broached the idea of SDS with families found that the prospect of the added responsibility involved was not always welcomed. It was thought that parents who felt overwhelmed by their situation and responsibilities valued others taking some responsibility from their shoulders, at least when support was first offered and confidence was low.

There are a limited number of studies and evaluations from across the UK which highlight both the benefits and the barriers to the SDS approach (Ridley *et al.*, 2011; Keilty, 2014). While some writers can see benefits in the approach, the conclusion of many is that much needs to be thought through before policies can be fully implemented in practice.

We hope that some of what parents told us, as reported in this book, might be of assistance in planning an SDS-led approach to family support services, given the intention to develop their use.

A final word

We know that it may not be feasible for practitioners to make use of all the practice suggestions we describe. We are aware that practitioners' roles differ, and most are working within significant constraints of time and resources. We do consider, however, that by thinking about the basic principles and the approaches, which parents tell us are important to them, and by using the time that is available wisely, particularly during the early stages of forming a relationship with them, that the support offered by practitioners can be effective – at least for some families. Skilled practice combined with humane personal qualities can make all the difference to a family:

> 'If you get a good person it really makes a difference.' Parent, study G

Perhaps what practitioners need to ask themselves is how they can become the 'good person' to a family they are supporting.

APPENDIX:

The research studies

The research studies were undertaken between 2004 and 2016, by Cheryl Burgess *et al.* from the Faculty of Social Sciences at the University of Stirling and researchers and practitioners from other institutions and agencies. The studies are listed in chronological order (see Figure A.1). Each one has a letter which is used for attributing quotes from the parents who participated in them.

Figure A.1: Individual study details

Study name, date and where undertaken	Service description and published reports
A Evaluation of Four Aberlour Childcare Trust Youth Crime Prevention Projects: National Parenting Development Project 1 2004–2006 *Scotland*	Direct parenting programme work and strategic development of parenting in multiple areas of Scotland. Burgess, C. and Walker, M. (2006) *Evaluation of the National Parenting Development Project*, Stirling: Aberlour Childcare Trust
B Evaluation of Four Aberlour Childcare Trust Youth Crime Prevention Projects: National Parenting Development Project 2 2006–2008 *Scotland*	Extension of the above evaluation covering two further years' work, including a parenting programme in HMP and YOI Cornton Vale, Scotland. Burgess, C. and Malloch, M. (2008) *Evaluation of the National Parenting Development Project*, Stirling: Aberlour Childcare Trust
C Evaluation of CHILDREN 1st 4Ward Steps Service in North Ayrshire 2010 *Scotland*	Extensive support for families with infants on the pre-birth Child Protection Register in North Ayrshire, Scotland. Burgess, C. (2010) ' "Small steps for big changes": Evaluation of the CHILDREN 1st 4ward Steps Family Support Service in North Ayrshire', Edinburgh: CHILDREN 1st
D Action Research with Aberlour Glasgow Bridges Family Support Service 2008–2011 *Scotland*	A family support service aimed at improving the education, health and well-being outcomes for children affected by parental substance misuse in north-east Glasgow, Scotland. Burgess, C (2011) *Glasgow Bridges: An Aberlour Family Service*, Stirling: Aberlour Childcare Trust

E Evaluation of Women in Focus Mentoring Scheme: South-West Scotland Criminal Justice Authority and Barnardo's 2009–2011 *Scotland*	A mentoring service for women involved with the criminal justice system in south-west Scotland. Burgess, C., Malloch, M. and McIvor, G. (2011) *Women in Focus: An Evaluation*, Glasgow: Scottish Centre for Crime and Justice Research
F Action on Neglect: A resource pack (with Action for Children) Economic and Social Research Council 2012–2013 *England*	A resource pack based on work with three local authority social services departments in England and input from a parent (and young people) consultative group. Burgess, C., Daniel, B., Whitfield, E., Derbyshire, D. and Taylor, J. (2013) *Action on Neglect: A Resource Pack*, University of Stirling and Action for Children. Economic and Social Research Council ES/JO1790.1
G UK Review of Child Neglect (with Action for Children) – third in the series focusing on children and parents' views – 2012–2014 *UK*	Year Three of a UK-wide review of child neglect involving focus groups with forty parents and thirty-eight children and young people. Burgess, C., Daniel, B, Scott, J., Dobbin, H., Mulley, K. and Whitfield, E. (2014) *Preventing Child Neglect in the UK: What Makes Services Accessible to Children and Families?*, Watford: Action for Children
H Evaluation of Public Social Partnership Early Years Intervention led by CHILDREN 1st 2013–2015 *Scotland*	An intensive family-support PSP model for families considered to be 'just coping' in five areas of Scotland. Burgess, C., Rigby, P. and Daniel, B. (2015b) *CHILDREN 1st Public Social Partnership Early Years Intervention Final Evaluation Report*, Edinburgh: CHILDREN 1st
J Evaluation of Public Social Partnership Early Years Intervention led by Quarriers 2014–2015 *Scotland*	An intensive family-support PSP model for families considered to be 'just coping' in North Ayrshire, Scotland. Burgess, C., Rigby, P. and Daniel, B. (2015a) *Together We Can: Helping Families in North Ayrshire PSP Family Support Service Evaluation Report*, Bridge of Weir: Quarriers
K Evaluation of A Good Start Programme for Midlothian Sure Start 2014–2015 *Scotland*	A baby massage and wider support programme for families of infants in Midlothian, Scotland. Burgess, C. and Stone, K (2015) *Midlothian Sure Start A Good Start Programme: Collaborative Research and Evaluation*, Dalkeith: Midlothian Sure Start
L Evaluation of Falkirk Children's Commission Child Protection Outcomes Framework 2012–2013 *Scotland*	A pilot of an outcomes framework for children with a Child Protection Plan in Falkirk Council area, including the views of parents. Burgess, C. and Stone, K. (2013) *Evaluation of a Pilot Outcomes Framework for Children on the Child Protection Register in Falkirk*, Falkirk: Falkirk Children's commission

M Nurture Corners in Glasgow City Council Early Years Centres 2015 *Scotland*	An exploration of the use of nurture approaches in Early Years centres in Glasgow, Scotland. Stephen, C., Stone, K., Burgess, C., Daniel, B. and Smith, J (2014) *Nurture Corners in Nurseries: Exploring Perspectives on Nurture Approaches in Pre-school Provision in Glasgow*, Glasgow: Glasgow Centre for Population Health
N Evaluation of Self-directed Support Pilot in Falkirk Council Children's Services 2015 *Scotland*	A pilot into the use of SDS (parents' views not included). Burgess, C. (2015) *Falkirk Council Self-directed Support Pilot: An Evaluation*, Falkirk: Falkirk Children's Commission
P Evaluation of Midlothian Sure Start Dads and Grandparents Service 2016 *Scotland*	A support service for fathers and grandparents. Stone, K. and Burgess, C. (2016) *Midlothian Sure Start's Dads and Grandparents Service. Evaluation Report*, Dalkeith: Midlothian Sure Start

References

Antcliff, G. (2010) 'Resilience practice framework: Assessing and promoting resilience in vulnerable children and families', Presentation for conference at Metro Central, Paddington, NSW: The Benevolent Society

Ashley, C. and Nixon, P. (eds) (2007) *Family Group Conferences: Where Next? Policies and Practices for the Future*, London: Family Rights Group

Asmussen, K. and Weizel, K. (2010) *Evaluating the Evidence: Fathers, Families and Children*, London: National Academy for Parenting Research

Barlow, J. (1999) 'What works in parent education programmes?', in Lloyd, E. (ed.) (1999) *Parenting Matters: What Works in Parent Education Programmes?*, Barkingside: Barnardos

Barnes, J., Ball, M., Meadows, P., Howden, B., Jackson, A., Henderson, J. and Niven, L. (2011) *The Family Nurse Partnership in England: Wave 1 Implementation in Toddlerhood and a Comparison between Waves 1 and 2a of Implementation in Pregnancy and Infancy*, London: Department of Health

Barrett, H. (2003) *Parenting Programmes for Families at Risk: A Source Book*, London: National Family and Parenting Institute

Baumrind, D. (1972) 'Socialisation and instrumental competence in young children', in Hartup, W. W. (ed.) (1972) *The Young Child: Reviews of Research*, Vol. 2, Washington, DC: National Association for the Education of Young Children

Belsky, J. (1984) 'The determinants of parenting: a process model', *Child Development*, Vol. 55, pp. 85–96

Belsky, J. (1993) 'Etiology of child maltreatment: A developmental-ecological analysis', *Psychological Bulletin*, Vol. 114, pp. 413–34

Bourdieu, Pierre (1986), 'The forms of capital', in Richardson, J. G. (ed.) (1986) *Handbook of Theory and Research for the Sociology of Education*, New York, NY: Greenwood

Brandon, M., Belderson, P., Warren, C., Howe, D., Gardner, R. and Dodsworth, J. (2008) *Analysing Child Deaths and Serious Injury Through Abuse and Neglect: What Can We Learn? A Biennial Analysis of Serious Case Reviews 2003–2005*, London: Department of Children, Schools and Families

Brandon, M., Sidebotham, P., Bailey, S., Belderson, P., Hawley, C., Ellis, C. and Megson, M. (2012) *New Learning from Serious Case Reviews: A Two Year Report for 2009–11*, London: Department for Education

Brofenbrenner, U. (1979) *The Ecology of Human Development*, Cambridge, MA: Harvard University Press

Brownlie, J., Anderson, S. and Ormston, R. (2006) *Children as Researchers*, Edinburgh: Scottish Executive

Buchanan, A. (2002) 'Family support', in McNeish, D., Newman, T. and Roberts, H. (eds) (2002) *What Works for Children? Effective Services for Children and Families*, Buckingham: Open University Press

Buckley, H. (2005) 'Neglect: No monopoly on expertise', in Taylor, J. and Daniel, B. (eds) (2005) *Child Neglect: Practice Issues for Health and Social Care*, London: Jessica Kingsley

Burgess, C. (2010) ' "Small steps for big changes": Evaluation of the CHILDREN 1st 4ward Steps Family Support Service in North Ayrshire', Edinburgh: CHILDREN 1st

Burgess, C (2011) *Glasgow Bridges: An Aberlour Family Service*, Stirling: Aberlour Childcare Trust

Burgess, C. (2015) *Falkirk Council Self-directed Support Pilot: An Evaluation*, Falkirk: Falkirk Children's Commission

Burgess, C., Daniel, B., Scott, J., Dobbin, H., Mulley, K. and Whitfield, E. (2014) *Preventing Child Neglect in the UK: What Makes Services Accessible to Children and Families?*, Watford: Action for Children

Burgess, C., Daniel, B., Whitfield, E., Derbyshire, D. and Taylor, J. (2013) *Action on Neglect: A Resource Pack*, University of Stirling and Action for Children Economic and Social Research Council ES/JO1790.1

Burgess, C. and Malloch, M. (2008) *Evaluation of the National Parenting Development Project*, Stirling: Aberlour Childcare Trust

Burgess, C., Malloch, M. and McIvor, G. (2011) *Women in Focus: An Evaluation*, Glasgow: Scottish Centre for Crime and Justice Research

Burgess, C., Rigby, P. and Daniel, B. (2015a) *Together We Can: Helping Families in North Ayrshire PSP Family Support Service Evaluation Report*, Bridge of Weir: Quarriers

Burgess, C., Rigby, P. and Daniel, B. (2015b) *CHILDREN 1st Public Social Partnership Early Years Intervention Final Evaluation Report*, Edinburgh: CHILDREN 1st

Burgess, C. and Stone, K. (2013) *Evaluation of a Pilot Outcomes Framework for Children on the Child Protection Register in Falkirk*, Falkirk: Falkirk Children's Commission

Burgess, C. and Stone, K (2015) *Midlothian Sure Start A Good Start Programme: Collaborative Research and Evaluation*, Dalkeith: Midlothian Sure Start

Burgess, C. and Walker, M. (2006) *Evaluation of the National Parenting Development Project*, Stirling: Aberlour Childcare Trust

Canavan, J., Pinkerton, J. and Dolan, P. (2016) *Understanding Family Support: Policy, Practice and Theory*, London: Jessica Kingsley

Care Inspectorate (2017) *Joint Inspection of Services for Children and Young People Inspection Handbook*, Dundee: Care Inspectorate

Clapton, G. (2013) *Social Work with Fathers: Positive Practice*, Edinburgh: Dunedin Academic Press

Clark, A. and Moss, P. (2016) *Listening to Young Children: The Mosaic Approach*, London: National Children's Bureau

Cleaver, H. (2001) 'When parents' issues influence their ability to respond to their children's needs', in Horwath, J. (ed.) (2001) *The Child's World: Assessing Children in Need*, London: Jessica Kingsley

Cohen, S. (2002) *Folk Devils and Moral Panics*, 3rd edn, London: Routledge

Coles, E., Cheyne, H. and Daniel, B. (2015) 'Early years interventions to improve child health and wellbeing: What works, for whom and in what circumstances? Protocol for a realist review', *Systematic Reviews*, Vol. 4, No. 79; doi:10.1186/

s13643–015–0068–5

Crosby, N., Kelly, G., Lazarus, C., Macintyre, L. and Sibthorp K. (2012) *Building a New Relationship with Children, Young People and Families*, Withall: In Control

Crosby, N. and Wheeler, J. (2010) *Exploring Self-directed Support and Signs of Safety*, Withall: In Control

Daly, K. J. (1996) *Families and Time: Keeping Pace in a Hurried Culture*, Newbury Park, CA: Sage

Daniel, B. and Rioch, C. (2007) 'Parenting issues and practice in child protection', in Wilson, K. and James, A. (eds) (2007) *The Child Protection Handbook*, 3rd edn, London: Bailliere Tindall

Daniel, B. and Taylor, J. (2005) 'Do they care? The role of fathers in cases of child neglect', in Taylor, J. and Daniel, B. (eds) (2005) *Child Neglect: Practice Issues for Health and Social Care*, London: Jessica Kingsley

Daniel, B., Taylor, J. and Scott, J. (2011) *Recognizing and Helping the Neglected Child: Evidence-based Practice for Assessment and Intervention*, London: Jessica Kingsley

Daniel, B., Vincent, S., Farrall, E. and Arney, F. (2009) 'How is the concept of resilience operationalised in practice with vulnerable children?', *International Journal of Child and Family Welfare*, Vol. 12, No. 1, pp. 2–21

Daniel, B. and Wassell, S. (2002a) *Adolescence: Assessing and Promoting Resilience in Vulnerable Children 1*, London: Jessica Kingsley

Daniel, B. and Wassell, S. (2002b) *The School Years: Assessing and Promoting Resilience in Vulnerable Children 2*, London: Jessica Kingsley

Daniel, B. and Wassell, S. (2002c) *The Early Years: Assessing and Promoting Resilience in Vulnerable Children 3*, London: Jessica Kingsley

Davies, C. and Ward, H. (1995) *Child Protection: Messages from Research*, London: Jessica Kingsley

Davies, C. and Ward, H. (2012) *Safeguarding Children across Services: Messages from Research*, London: Jessica Kingsley

Day, L., Bryson, C., White, C., Purdon, S., Bewley, H., Kirchner Sala, L. and Portes, J. (2016) *National Evaluation of the Troubled Families Programme: Final Synthesis Report*, London: Department for Communities and Local Government

Department of Health (2000) *Framework for the Assessment of Children in Need and Their Families in England and Wales*, London: HMSO

Department of Health (2003) *Every Child Matters*, London: HMSO

Department for Work and Pensions (2017) *Improving Lives: Helping Workless Families*, London: Department for Work and Pensions

Dolan, P., Pinkerton, J. and Canavan, J. (2006) *Family Support as Reflective Practice*, London: Jessica Kingsley

Donkin, A. (2014) *Good-Quality Parenting Programmes and the Home to School Transition*, London: Institute of Health Equity and Public Health England

Emond, R., Steckley, L. and Roesch-Marsh, A. (2016) *Therapeutic Child Care: What You Need to Know to Create a Healing Home*, London: Jessica Kingsley

Erickson, J. and Henderson, A. (1998) 'Diverging realities: Abused women and their children', in Campbell, J. (ed.) (1998) *Empowering Survivors of Abuse: Health Care for Battered Women and Their Children*, London: Sage

FaHCSIA (2009) *Father-inclusive Practice Guide: A Tool to Support the Inclusion of*

Fathers in a Holistic Approach to Service Delivery, Canberra: Australian Government Department of Families, Housing, Community Service and Indigenous Affairs, Commonwealth of Australia

Family Rights Group (2011) *Working with Risky Fathers*, London: Family Rights Group

Featherstone, B. (2009) *Contemporary Fathering: Theory, Policy and Practice*, Bristol: Policy Press

Ferguson, H. (2010) 'Walks, home visits and atmospheres: Risk and the everyday practices and mobilities of social work and child protection', *British Journal of Social Work*, Vol. 40, No. 4 (June), pp. 1100–17

Fox Harding, L. (1997) *Perspectives in Child Care Policy*, 2nd edn, London: Longman

Friborg, O., Hjemdal, O., Rosenvinge, J. H. and Martinussen, M. (2003) 'A new rating scale for adult resilience: What are the central protective resources behind healthy adjustment?', *International Journal of Methods in Psychiatric Research*, Vol. 12, pp. 65–76

Ghate, D., Shaw, C. and Hazel, N. (2000) *Fathers and Family Centres: Engaging Fathers in Preventive Services*, York: Joseph Rowntree Foundation

Gibbs, J. (2009). 'Changing the cultural story in child protection: Learning from the insider's experience', *Child and Family Social Work*, Vol. 14, No. 3, pp. 289–99

Gibbs, J., Dwyer, J. and Vivekananda, K. (2009) *Leading Practice: A Resource Guide for Child Protection Middle Managers*, Melbourne: Victorian Government Department of Human Services

Gilligan, R. (2001a) *Promoting Resilience*, London: British Agencies for Adoption and Fostering

Gilligan, R. (2001b) 'Promoting positive outcomes for children in need: The assessment of protective factors', in Horwath, J. (ed.) (2001) *The Child's World: Assessing Children in Need*, London: Jessica Kingsley

Gilligan, R. (2009) 'Positive turning points in the dynamics of change over the life course', in Mancini, J. A. and Roberto, K. A. (eds) (2009) *Pathways of Human Development: Explorations of Change*, Lanham, MD: Lexington Books

Hart, A. and Aumann, K. (2017) *Building Child and Family Resilience – Boing Boing's Resilience Approach in Action: Frontline Briefing*, Dartington: Research in Practice

Helm, D. (2011) 'Judgements or assumptions? The role of analysis in assessing children and young people's needs', *British Journal of Social Work*, Vol. 41, No. 5, pp. 894–911

Hill, M., Stafford, A., Seaman, P., Ross, N. and Daniel, B. (2007) *Parenting and Resilience*, York: Joseph Rowntree Foundation

HM Government (2015) *Information Sharing: Advice for Practitioners Providing Safeguarding Services to Children, Young People, Parents and Carers*, London: Department for Education

Holloway, S. L. and Pimlott-Wilson, H. (2014) ' "Any advice is welcome isn't it?" Neoliberal parenting education, local mothering cultures, and social class', *Environment and Planning*, Vol. 46, pp. 94–111

Holman, B., Parker, R. and Utting, W. (1999) *Reshaping Child Care Practice*, London: National Social Work Institute

Horwath, J. (2001) *The Child's World: Assessing Children in Need*, London: Jessica Kingsley, pp. 23–34

Horwath, J. (2005) 'Is this child neglect? The influences of differences in perceptions of child neglect on social work practice', in Taylor, J. and Daniel, B. (eds) (2005) *Child Neglect: Practice Issues for Health and Social Care*, London: Jessica Kingsley

Horwath, J. (2013) *Child Neglect: Planning and Intervention*, Basingstoke: Palgrave Macmillan

Horwath, J. and Morrison, T. (2001) 'Assessment of parental motivation to change', in Horwath, J. (ed.) (2001) *The Child's World: Assessing Children in Need*, London: Jessica Kingsley

Jack, G. (2000) 'Ecological influences on parenting and child development', *British Journal of Social Work*, Vol. 30, pp. 703–20

Jack, G. and Jordan, B. (1999) 'Social capital and child welfare', *Children and Society*, Vol. 13, pp. 242–56

Jones, D. (2010) 'Assessment of parenting', in Horwath, J. (ed.) (2010) *The Child's World: Assessing Children in Need*, London: Jessica Kingsley

Kazi, M. (2003) *Realist Evaluation in Practice*, Thousand Oaks, CA: Sage

Keilty, T. (2014) *Self-directed Support and Early Intervention*, Withall: In Control

Kellett, J. and Apps, J. (2009) *Assessments of Parenting and Parenting Support Need: A Study of Four Professional Groups*, York: Joseph Rowntree Foundation

Kosonen, M. (2011) *Getting it Right: Report on Angus Learning Partnership for Children Affected by Parental Substance Misuse (CAPSM)*, Edinburgh: Scottish Government.

Lewis, C. and Lamb, M. (2007) *Understanding Fatherhood: A Review of Recent Research*, York: Joseph Rowntree Foundation

Lindsay, G. and Cullen, A. M. (2011) *Evaluation of the Parenting Early Intervention Programme*, London: Department for Education

Luthar, S. (2003) *Resilience and Vulnerability*, New York, NY: Cambridge University Press

Luthar, S. (2005) 'Resilience in development: A synthesis of research across five decades', in Cicchetti, D. and Cohen, D. J. (eds) (2005) *Development Psychopathology: Risk, Disorder and Adaptation*, 2nd edn, Vol. 3, New York, NY: Wiley

McCabe, A. and Horsley, K. (2008) *The Evaluator's Cookbook: Exercises for Participatory Evaluation with Children and Young People*, London: Routledge

McCubbin, H. I., Hamilton, I., Thompson, E. A., Thompson, A. I. and Futrell, J. A. (1999) *The Dynamics of Resilient Families*, Thousand Oaks, CA: Sage

McDonald, L., Miller, H. and Sandler, J. (2015). 'A social ecological, relationship-based strategy for parent involvement: Families And Schools Together (FAST)', *Journal of Children's Services*, Vol. 1, pp. 218–30

Marryat, L. L. T., McGranachan, M., Barry, S., Sim, F., White, J. and Wilson, P. (2014) *Parenting Support Framework Evaluation Final Report*, Glasgow: NHS Greater Glasgow and Clyde

Maxwell, N., Scourfield, J., Featherstone, B., Holland, S. and Tolman, R. (2012) 'Engaging fathers in child welfare services: A narrative review of recent research evidence', *Child and Family Social Work*, Vol. 17, No. 4, pp. 160–9

Milner, J. and O'Byrne, P. (2002) *Assessment in Social Work*, 2nd edn, Basingstoke:

Palgrave Macmillan

Moran, P., Ghate, D. and van der Merwe, A. (2004) *What Works in Parenting Support? A Review of the International Literature, Research Report 574*, London: Department for Education and Skills

Morrison, T. (2005) *Staff Supervision in Social Care: Making a Real Difference for Staff and Service Users*, Brighton: Pavilion

Munro, E. (2011) *The Munro Review of Child Protection Final Report: A Child-Centred System*, London: The Stationery Office

Northern Ireland Executive (2011) *Understanding the Needs of Children in Northern Ireland (UNOCiNI)*, Belfast: Northern Ireland Executive

Northern Ireland Executive (2014) *Delivering Social Change for Children and Young People*, Belfast: Northern Ireland Executive

NSPCC (2013) *Assessing Parenting Capacity: An NSPCC factsheet*, London: NSPCC

OECD (2011) *Doing Better for Families* Research Programme, Paris: Organisation for Economic Co-operation and Development. Available from URL: www.oecd.org/social/family/47849499.pdf (accessed 19 January 2018)

Ofsted (2017) *Inspecting Local Authority Children's Services: Guidance for Inspectors*, London: HMSO

Olds, D. L. (2006) 'The nurse-family partnership: An evidence-based prevention intervention', *Infant Mental Health Journal*, Vol. 27, pp. 5–25

Paavilainen, E., Astedt–Kurki, P. and Paunonen, M. (2000) 'School nurses operational modes and ways of collaborating in caring for child abusing families in Finland', *Journal of Clinical Nursing*, Vol. 9, No. 5, pp. 742–50

Pawson, R. and Tilley, N. (2007) *Realist Evaluation*, London: Sage

Payne, M. (2005) *Modern Social Work Theory*, 3rd edn, Basingstoke: Palgrave Macmillan

Platt, D. Riches, K., and Helm, D. (2016) 'C-Change Capacity to Change Assessment Manual – Scottish version' (online), School for Policy Studies, University of Bristol. Available from URL: www.bristol.ac.uk/media-library/sites/sps/documents/c-change/C-Change_SCOTTISH_Digital_ISBN.pdf (accessed 5 January 2018)

Quinton, D. (2004) *Supporting Parents: Messages from Research*, London: Jessica Kingsley

Quinton, D. and Rutter, M. (1988) *Parenting Breakdown*, London: Department of Health and Social Services

Reder, P. and Lucey, C. (1995) 'Significant issues in the assessment of parenting', in Reder, P. and Lucey, C. (eds) (1995) *Assessment of Parenting: Psychiatric and Psychological Contributions*, London: Routledge

Ridley, J., Spandler, H., Rosengard, A., Little, S., Cornes, M., Manthorpe, J., Hunter, S., Kinder, T. and Gray, B. (2011) *Evaluation of Self-directed Support Test Sites in Scotland*, Edinburgh: Scottish Parliament

Rose, N. (1989) *Governing the Soul: The Shaping of the Private Self*, London: Routledge

RQIA (2016) *Guidance for Regulated Service Providers*, Belfast: Regulation and Quality Improvement Authority

Russell, C. (2009) 'Communities in control: Community asset-building', European

Asset-based Community Development Conference Paper, Liverpool

Sammons, P., Hall, J., Smees, R. and Goff, J. with Sylva, K., Smith, T., Evangelou, M., Eisenstadt, N. and Smith, G. (2015) *The Impact of Children's Centres: Studying the effects of Children's Centres in Promoting Better Outcomes for Young Children and Their Families – Evaluation of Children's Centres in England (ECCE, Strand 4)*, London: Department for Education

Sawyer, E. and Burton, S. (2016) *A Practical Guide to Early Intervention and Family Support Assessing Needs and Building Resilience in Families Affected by Parental Mental Health Problems or Substance Misuse*, London: National Children's Bureau

SCIE (2015) *Co-production in Social Care: What Is It and How to Do It?*, London: Social Care Institute for Excellence

Scottish Government (2008) *A Guide to Getting it Right for Every Child*, Edinburgh: Scottish Government

Scottish Government (2009) *The Early Years Framework*, Edinburgh: Scottish Government

Scottish Government (2010) *Self-directed Support: A National Strategy for Scotland*, Edinburgh: Scottish Government

Scottish Government (2011) *A Practical Guide to Forming and Operating Public Social Partnerships*, Edinburgh: Scottish Government

Scottish Government (2012) *A Guide to Getting it Right for Every Child*, Edinburgh: Scottish Government

Scourfield, J., Cheung, S. Y. and Macdonald, G. (2014) 'Working with fathers to improve children's well-being: Results of a survey exploring service provision and intervention approach in the UK', *Children and Youth Services Review*, Vol. 43, pp. 40–50

Shemmings, Y. and Shemmings, D. (1996) 'Building trust when making enquiries', in Platt, D. and Shemmings, D. (eds) (1996) *Making Enquiries into Alleged Child Abuse and Neglect: Partnership with Families*, Chichester: John Wiley

Shemmings, Y. and Shemmings, D. (2001) 'Empowering children and family members to participate in the assessment process', in Howarth, J. (ed.))2001) *The Child's World: Assessing Children in Need*, London: Jessica Kingsley

Slasberg, C., Beresford, P. and Schofield, P. (2012) 'How self-directed support is failing to deliver personal budgets and personalisation', *Research, Policy and Planning*, Vol. 29, No. 3, pp. 161–77

Stafford, A., Parton, N., Vincent, S. and Smith, C. (2012) *Child Protection Systems in the United Kingdom: A Comparative Analysis*, London: Jessica Kingsley

Statham, J. and Biehal, N. (2005) *Supporting Families*, Research and Practice Briefing, Vol. 11. Available from URL: https://pure.york.ac.uk/portal/en/publications/supporting-families(14175e35-95f0-4119-b4dd-2a476de5ed42).html (accessed 19 January 2018)

Stephen, C., Stone, K., Burgess, C., Daniel, B. and Smith, J (2014) *Nurture Corners in Nurseries: Exploring Perspectives on Nurture Approaches in Pre-school Provision in Glasgow*, Glasgow: Glasgow Centre for Population Health

Stone, K. and Burgess, C. (2016) *Midlothian Sure Start's Dads and Grandparents Service. Evaluation Report*, Dalkeith: Midlothian Sure Start

Svrivastava, O. P., Fountain, R., Ayre, P. and Stewart, J. (2003) 'The graded care profile: A measure of care', in Calder, M. and Hackett, S. (eds) (2003) *Assessment in Child Care*, Dorset: Russell House

Tait, A. and Wosu, H. (2013) *Direct Work with Vulnerable Children: Playful Activities and Strategies for Communication*, London: Jessica Kingsley

Taylor, J. and Daniel, B. (eds) (2005) *Child Neglect: Practice Issues for Health and Social Care*, London: Jessica Kingsley

Thoburn, J., Lewis, A. and Shemmings, D. (1995) *Paternalism or Partnership? Family Involvement in the Child Protection Process*, London: HMSO

Trinder, L. (2000) 'A critical appraisal of evidence-based practice,' in Trinder, L. and Reynolds, S. (eds) (2000) *Evidence-based Practice: A Critical Appraisal*, Oxford: Blackwell Science

Turnell, A. and Edwards, S. (1999) *Signs of Safety: A Safety and Solution-orientated Approach to Child Protection Casework*, New York, NY: Norton

Vincent, S. (2010) 'An overview of safeguarding and protecting children across the UK', in Stafford, A., Vincent, S. and Parton, N. (eds) (2010) *Child Protection Reform across the UK*, Edinburgh: Dunedin Academic Press

Vincent, S. (2015) *Early Intervention: Supporting and Strengthening Families*, Edinburgh: Dunedin Academic Press

Walker, M., Glasgow, M. and Lacey, S. (2005) *Supporting Children by Getting Alongside Families: A Practice Guide Based on the Experience of Quarriers Family Resource Centre*, Bridge of Weir: Quarriers

Walsh, F. (1998) *Strengthening Family Resilience*, New York, NY: Guildford Press

Wilson, S. and Milne, E. J. (2013) *Young People Creating Belonging: Creative Sensory Methods to Explore How Young People Who Are Looked After Feel That They Belong*, Glasgow: Institute for Research and Innovation in Social Sciences

Yates, T. M. and Masten, A. (2004) 'Prologue: The promise of resilience research for policy and practice', in Newman, T. (ed.) (2004) *What Works in Building Resilience?*, Barkingside: Barnardos

INDEX

ACASI (Audio Computer-Assisted Self-Interviewing) 98
ACES (Active Children Eating Smart) 79
Action for Children, Family Partners 9
Active Children Eating Smart (ACES) 79
adult literacy help 84
alcohol problems 54, 61
Antcliff, G. 106
anxiety
  assessment 35
  children 79
  defensiveness 22–3
  and depression 62, 68, 78–9, 84, 95
  feeling inadequate 66, 74
  going out 64–5, 69
  home concerns 63
  meeting practitioners 23, 24–9, 31
  new situations 25, 30
  social network 81
  talking with others 65
Apps, J. 43
art and craft classes 69
Ashley, C. 108
Assessing and Promoting Resilience in Children 50
Assessing Parenting Capacity, NSPCC 43
assessment xviii–xix
  anxiety 35
  child welfare 42–3, 51
  family support practitioners 33–8
  fathers 35–6, 52
  frameworks 38–41, 52
  language used 36–8, 50, 52

  multi-agency 11, 38, 92–3, 94
  parenting 39–40, 42–50
  resilience-based approach 38
assessment paralysis 34
Audio Computer-Assisted Self-Interviewing (ACASI) 98
Aumann, K. 7
austerity measures viii

baby's clothing grants 77
baby's withdrawal symptoms 59
Barnes, J. 10
Baumrind, D. 39
bedtime routines 70
Belsky, J. 5
Benefits Agency 78
Biehal, N. 10, 12
blob tree 49
board games 69, 83
'Boing Boing' project 7
Bourdieu, P. 7–8
Brandon, M. 39
briefing materials 103
Brofenbrenner, U. 5
Buchanan, A. xiv
Buckley, H. 15
budget cuts 14
budgeting 71–2, 78
bullying 95
Burgess, C. 15, 98, 108, 111–13
Burns, H. 86
Burton, S. xvii–xviii

Canavan, J. xiii, 8
  Understanding Family Support 3
capacity to change 39, 73
Care Act, England and Wales 108
carers x–xi, xv–xvi
C-Change 39
changes 39, 55, 73, 75, 101
  see also capacity to change

child development 61–2
child protection 11, 14, 15, 38, 102
Child Protection Register 108
child welfare 14, 42–3, 50–1
childcare 15, 84–5
childcare books 58
children
    activities offered 73, 100
    anxiety 79
    home visits 27, 29
    needs recognised 67
    parent's imprisonment 64
    taken into care 54–5, 73
    views on family support xii,
        98–101
Children and Young People
    (Scotland) Act 107
children's centres 12
Children's Programme 107
children's rights 15
Citizens' Advice Bureaux 78
Clark, A. xvii
class factors 14, 41
Cleaver, H. 42
Cohen, S. 14
Coles, E. 90
communication 13, 67–8, 82–3
Community Payback 77
community safety 78
community-asset building 86
community-based activities 85–6
competitiveness 69
compliance 39
confidence 13, 74
    building of 53, 64–7, 67–72, 78,
        85, 107–8, 109
    dealing with agencies 54
    depression 66, 78
    of family support practitioners
        103, 104
    in family support practitioners
        59
    from friendship 80–1
    lack of 58–9
    as tenants 77–8
cooking 71–2
coping skills 6, 13, 76

co-production 108
Crosby, N. 107

Daly, K. J. 8
Daniel, B. 7, 10, 13, 18, 19, 35, 36,
    39, 41, 50, 83
Davies, C. 10, 12, 18, 40, 53
Day, L. xvii, 12, 14
debt avoidance 78
defensiveness xiii, 22, 23, 26, 66
*Delivering Social Change for Children
    and Young People* (Northern
    Ireland Executive) xvii
Department for Work and Pensions:
    *Improving Lives: Helping Workless
    Families* xvii
Department of Health
    Every Child Matters 11
    *The Framework for Assessment
        of Children in Need and Their
        Families in England and Wales*
        39, 43
depression
    and anxiety 62, 68, 78–9, 84, 95
    communication 68
    confidence 66, 78
    environment 54
    housing 54, 77
    lessened 79, 109
    lone father 22
    mother 62, 84, 95
    neglect 65
    parents 19
    self-esteem 65
developmental milestones ladder 47
difficulties, temporary 54–5
disability, people with xi
disruptive families 14
dissent 39
Doing Better for Families (OECD) xi
Dolan, P. xiv
domestic violence 7, 65
drug misuse
    impact on child 61–2
    maternal 59, 64
    parents xi, 10, 54, 66, 79, 95, 96–7

early childhood play xv
early intervention xiii–xiv, 22–3, 90
The Early Years Framework (Scottish
    Government) xvii
Early Years staff xvi
ecological theory ix, 3, 5–6, 15
eco-map 47
education for parents 83–5
Edwards, S. 38
Emond, R. xvii
emotion cards 47
emotional intelligence 49, 50, 54
emotional literacy 63–4, 82–3
emotional support/practical help 59
emotional well-being 62–3
empowerment 37, 107–8, 109
England: 'Troubled Families'
    progamme xvii
England and Wales
    Care Act 108
    Every Child Matters 11
environmental influence 54
Erickson, J. 6
Every Child Matters 11
everyday life 45, 46, 54, 70

Families and Schools Together
    (FAST) 10
family
    assessed 33–5
    outside the home 24–6
    and social workers 11
    varieties of x–xi
    see also Troubled Families
        Initiative; vulnerable families
Family Group Conferencing 108
family learning 72, 83–4
Family Network Meeting 108
Family Nurse Partnership Model
    9–10, 11–12
family outcomes framework 95–7
Family Partners, Action for Children
    9
family resilience theory ix, 3, 6–8,
    15, 75–6, 87
Family Rights Group 36
family rooms 25

family support x, xiii–xiv
    children's views xii, 98–101
    effectiveness xix, 11–13, 89–90,
        101
    first meetings 23–9
    future practice developments 106
    health visitors 10–11, 19
    long-term 87
    models 9–10, 15–16
    political perspective 14–15
    response to x, xvii–xix, 73
    social policy 14–15
family support practitioners xviii
    assessment 33–8
    confidence in 59
    confidence of 103, 104
    families outside the home 24–6
    fathers 56–7
    first meeting parents 23, 24–9, 31
    gender factors 57
    and health visitors 59
    home visits 26–9, 31
    knowledge 103–4
    learning 103–5, 107
    manner and approach 73–4
    outcomes 88–9
    and parents 9, 17–18, 37, 55–6,
        70, 106
    resilience 105–6
    support for 102–3, 104–5
    theoretical frameworks 2–3
    training courses 103
Family Support Service, Glasgow 26
family support services xii
    austerity measures viii
    child protection 14, 15
    continuing support 79–80
    denied 35
    effectiveness 88–90, 101
    parent–school relationship 21,
        48–9, 72
    response to 102
Family tree 47
FAST (Families and Schools
    Together) 10
fathers xv–xvi, 29, 35–6, 52, 56–7,
    60, 100

fathers' group 85–6
Ferguson, H. 26
Finland, school nurses 13
first meetings 23–9, 31
flexibility 13, 45
food preparation 62–3, 71–2, 79
Fox Harding, L. 15
*The Framework for Assessment of
  Children in Need and Their Families
  in England and Wales* (Dept of
  Health) 39, 43
Friborg, O. 6
friendships 80–1
gardening 81

gender factors 57
Getting it Right for Every Child: see
  GIRFEC
Gibbs, J. 105–6
Gilligan, R. 7, 8, 81
GIRFEC *(Getting it Right for Every
  Child)* 4, 11, 14–15, 21, 38, 107
Glasgow Family Support Service 26
Goodmans Strengths and Difficulties
  Questionnaire 94, 95, 97
government policies xvi–xvii
GPs (general practitioners) 19, 21,
  22, 29, 78, 95, 96
Graded Care Profile 38
grants for baby's clothing 77
gym sessions 79

hands-on approach 61
Hart, A. 7, 85
Health and Social Care Trusts, NI
  107
health centres 25
health quiz 49
health visitors 10–11, 19, 59
Helm, D. 50
helping services 25, 32, 41
Henderson, A. 6
heuristic play 69
Hill, M. 7, 13, 76
Holman, B. 25
home visits 27, 29, 31
Horwath, J. 37, 39, 40, 41
house drawings 48

House picture exercise 46
housing xvi, 14, 54, 77, 92

*Improving Lives: Helping Workless
  Families* (Dept for Work and
  Pensions) xvii
'In Control' 106–7
The Incredible Years 11, 60
inequality xvi, 8
information-sharing 38
interference 18–19, 22, 26–7
Internet resources 29, 58, 103
interventions 2–3, 18–19, 39, 105
  see also early intervention

Jack, G. 3, 5, 8, 81
Jones, D. 43
Jordan, B. 8
'just coping' families 108, 112

Kazi, M. 90
Keeling, Scarlett 41
Keilty, T. 107, 110
Kellett, J. 43
knowledge, need for 53, 57–9, 61–2,
  103–4
Kosonen, M. 21

language used 28, 36–8, 50, 52
learning
  communities of 7
  encouraging 72, 96
  enjoyable and useful 60–1, 62,
    72, 84
  play 68–9
  practical application 53
  for practitioners 103–5, 107
  shared 84
  styles of 58, 61, 74
  see also family learning
life events snake 47
Life Events Timeline 47
life-story work 62
listening skills 28
local authorities 11, 14–15, 21–2
Lucey, C. 34, 39
Luthar, S. 6, 8

McCann, Madeleine 41
McCubbin, H. I. 7
McDonald, L. 10
managerial structures 11, 89
Measuring Progress framework 108
mediating agencies 54
Mellow Parenting 11, 60
mental health 54, 78
    see also depression
middle class norms 14
Milner, J. 42, 50
money problems xvi, 54, 63, 69, 78
moral panics 14
Moran, P. xv, 12, 90–1, 92, 98
morning routines 70
Morrison, T. 39, 105
Moss, P. xvii
multi-agency assessment 11, 38,
    92–3, 94
Munro, E. 11, 15, 24, 56, 102
My World Triangle 38

National Society for Prevention of
    Cruelty to Children (NSPCC) 43
needs recognised 67, 96–7
neglect
    Action on Neglect 112
    capacity to change 39
    child protection 38
    depression 65
    experience of 62, 69–70
    fear of judgement 70
    identifying 4
    research on 98–9
    Review of Child Neglect 112
    risk of 73
network tree 49
Nixon, P. 108
Northern Ireland, Health and Social
    Care Trusts 107
Northern Ireland Executive
    *Delivering Social Change for
    Children and Young People* xvii
    UNO-CiNI 11
NSPCC (National Society for
    Prevention of Cruelty to Children):
    Assessing Parenting Capacity 43

Nurse Family Partnership 9–10
nurseries 22, 25, 29–30, 70, 72, 84,
    92

O'Byrne, P. 42, 50
OECD: *Doing Better for Families* xi
Olds, D. L. 14
open communication styles 13
open-mindedness 24, 42, 103
Our Day clock 40, 44, 45–6
'our family's wider world' 49–50
outcome indicators 91
outcomes 88–9, 91, 92–6, 101
outcomes frameworks 89–92, 94,
    101
Outcomes Star 46, 94, 97

Paavilainen, E. 13
paperwork, avoidance of 28
Parent cards 47
parenting xiii, xv
    children's views 98
    confidence 64–7
    defensiveness xiii, 22–3, 26, 66
    future 101
    good enough 41
    middle class norms 14
    styles 39
    see also skills in parenting
parenting assessment 39–40, 42–50
    bringing up children 47–8
    developmental milestones ladder
        47
    everyday life 46
    'getting to know' 46–7
    'my child' 48–9
    'our family's wider world' 49–50
    visual tools 44–5
Parenting Daily Hassles (PDH)
    questionnaire 94, 95, 97
parenting programmes 9–10, 60, 61
parenting task snap cards 47–8
parents viii–ix, x–xi, xvi, xvii–xix
    actively seeking help 17, 18–20,
        21
    alcohol problems 54, 61
    art and craft classes 69

on assessment xviii–xix, 34, 50
capacity to change 39
and children 5, 64
confidence lacking 58–9
drug misuse 61–2, 79, 95, 96–7
education for 83–5
empowerment 37
essential needs 54–5
and family support practitioners
    9, 17–18, 37, 53, 55–6, 70, 106
help offered 21–3
knowledge, need for 57–9
motivation 39–40
outcomes 91–2
own childhoods 57, 62, 64–5,
    68–9, 99
own schooldays 72, 84
personality/psychological well-
    being 5
in prison 64
with problems 19–20
schools 21, 48–9, 72
and social workers 26, 108–9
see also anxiety; depression
Pawson, R. 90
Payne, M. 2–3
PDH (Parenting Daily Hassles)
    questionnaire 94, 95, 97
peer support 86
Pit and ladder exercise 46
Platt, D. 39
playing outside 78
playing with children xv, xvii–xviii,
    68–9
Positive Parenting Programme
    (Triple P) 60
practical action xi–xii, 1–3, 28–9,
    31, 74
practical help 59, 67
practice development 89
practice wisdom 12
practice-based books xvii–xviii
problem-centred coping 13
Public Social Partnerships (PSP)
    108

qualitative research 12

Quarriers Family Support Service 9
questionnaires 94, 95
Quinton, D. 5, 12, 53

Reder, P. 34, 39
reflective practice 3, 89
resilience
    in children 6–7
    development of 81
    family support practiioners
        105–6
    social support networks 7–8
    sustainability 86
resilience-based approach ix, 3, 6,
    13, 38, 75–6
Resiliency Model of Family Stress,
    Adjustment and Adaptation 7
Resource Guide for Child Protection
    Managers (Gibbs) 105–6
Ridley, J. 110
Rioch, C. 10
role-modelling 71, 82, 105
Rose, N. 14
Russell, C. 86
Rutter, M. 5

safeguarding children's welfare 4, 27,
    30–1, 33–5, 55, 91
Sammons, P. 12
Sawyer, E. xvii–xviii
school nurses, Finland 13
schools
    attendance 82, 95
    environment 83–4
    and parents 19, 21, 48–9, 72
SCIE (Social Care Institute for
    Excellence) 103, 108
Scottish Government
    The Early Years Framework xvii
    GIRFEC 4, 11, 14–15, 21, 38, 107
    SDS approach 107
    SHANARRI well-being indicators
        62
SDQs (Strengths and Difficulties
    Questionnaire) 94, 95, 97
SDS (self-directed support) 106–10
security 77, 78, 87

self-determination 107–8
self-directed support (SDS) 106–10
self-efficacy ix, 87
self-esteem xv, 64–5, 84
Serious Case Reviews 55
shadowing 105
SHANARRI well-being indicators 62
Shemmings, Y. & D. 37
shopping 71–2
Signs of Safety 38, 107
skills in parenting
   confidence 53, 65–6, 67–72, 74
   encouragement 68
   for everyday life 46
   knowledge 57, 67–72
   reinforcing 58–9
Slasberg, C. 107
social capital 3, 7–8
Social Care Institute for Excellence (SCIE) 103, 108
Social Care (Self-directed Support) (Scotland) Act 107
social ecology 3
social network 8, 81, 85–6
social policy 14–15
social support 3, 7–8, 80–1
social work 2, 25
social workers
   child protection 102
   and families 11
   local authorities 11, 14–15, 21–2
   and parents 26, 108–9
   SDS 109
   and teachers 41
Stafford, A. 14, 15
Statham, J. 10, 12
Stone, K. 15
Strengths and Difficulties Questionnaire (SDQ) 94, 95, 97
strengths-based approach 13
stress
   coping with 7, 13, 34, 91
   everyday life 45–6
   families/practitioners xiv
   first meetings 23
   helping with homework 84

minimising 4, 5, 6, 55
money problems 63
for practitioner 103
routines 70
social networks 8
support by phone 70–1, 86
support planning 50, 51, 54–5
Supporting Families (Statham & Biehal) 12
Sure Start 12, 30
sustainability
   changes 73, 75, 77, 79, 83–4, 87
   family learning 83
   improvements 15, 91
   joining local groups 85
   lapsing 39, 83–4
   and resilience 86
   training for parents 72
Svrivastava, O. P. 38

Tait, A. xvii
taking children into care 54–5, 73
Taylor, J. 36, 39
teachers 41, 100
teenagers' self-worth xv
theoretical frameworks xviii, 1–3, 15
Thorburn, J. 37
ticking boxes 35
Tilley, N. 90
tokenism 39
training opportunities 83–5
Trinder, L. 92
Triple P (Positive Parenting Programme) 60
Troubled Families Initiative xvii, 12, 15–16
Turnell, A. 38

Understanding Family Support (Canavan) 3
UNO-CiNI 11

videos/practical help 67
Viewpoint 98
Vincent, S. 20
visual tools 44–5, 52, 101
Vox Liminis 72

vulnerable families xiv, xvii, 14, 105

waiting rooms 25
Walker, M. 12
Ward, H. 10, 12, 18, 40, 53
Wassell, S. 7, 50, 83

welfare benefits 14, 16
well-being 62–3, 85
Well-being Web 94–5
Wheeler, J. 107
work opportunities 83–5
Wosu, H. xvii